C000127856

The Cuckold's Chronicle: Being Select Trials for Adultry. Incest, Imbecility, Ravishment, &c.

Anonymous

The Cuckold's Chronicle: Being Select Trials for Adultry. Incest, Imbecility, Ravishment, &c.
The Cuckold's Chronicle: being Select Trials for Adultery, Incest, Imbecility, Ravishment, &c - 1798
HAR05712
Monograph
Harvard Law School Library
Boston: Printed for Those Who Choose to Purchase. 1798

The Making of Modern Law collection of legal archives constitutes a genuine revolution in historical legal research because it opens up a wealth of rare and previously inaccessible sources in legal, constitutional, administrative, political, cultural, intellectual, and social history. This unique collection consists of three extensive archives that provide insight into more than 300 years of American and British history. These collections include:

Legal Treatises, 1800-1926: over 20,000 legal treatises provide a comprehensive collection in legal history, business and economics, politics and government.

Trials, 1600-1926: nearly 10,000 titles reveal the drama of famous, infamous, and obscure courtroom cases in America and the British Empire across three centuries.

Primary Sources, 1620-1926: includes reports, statutes and regulations in American history, including early state codes, municipal ordinances, constitutional conventions and compilations, and law dictionaries.

These archives provide a unique research tool for tracking the development of our modern legal system and how it has affected our culture, government, business – nearly every aspect of our everyday life. For the first time, these high-quality digital scans of original works are available via print-on-demand, making them readily accessible to libraries, students, independent scholars, and readers of all ages.

old books. new life.

The BiblioLife Network

This project was made possible in part by the BiblioLife Network (BLN), a project aimed at addressing some of the huge challenges facing book preservationists around the world. The BLN includes libraries, library networks, archives, subject matter experts, online communities and library service providers. We believe every book ever published should be available as a high-quality print reproduction; printed on-demand anywhere in the world. This insures the ongoing accessibility of the content and helps generate sustainable revenue for the libraries and organizations that work to preserve these important materials.

The following book is in the "public domain" and represents an authentic reproduction of the text as printed by the original publisher. While we have attempted to accurately maintain the integrity of the original work, there are sometimes problems with the original work or the micro-film from which the books were digitized. This can result in minor errors in reproduction. Possible imperfections include missing and blurred pages, poor pictures, markings and other reproduction issues beyond our control. Because this work is culturally important, we have made it available as part of our commitment to protecting, preserving, and promoting the world's literature.

GUIDE TO FOLD-OUTS MAPS and OVERSIZED IMAGES

The book you are reading was digitized from microfilm captured over the past thirty to forty years. Years after the creation of the original microfilm, the book was converted to digital files and made available in an online database.

In an online database, page images do not need to conform to the size restrictions found in a printed book. When converting these images back into a printed bound book, the page sizes are standardized in ways that maintain the detail of the original. For large images, such as fold-out maps, the original page image is split into two or more pages

Guidelines used to determine how to split the page image follows:

• Some images are split vertically; large images require vertical and horizontal splits.
• For horizontal splits, the content is split left to right.
• For vertical splits, the content is split from top to bottom.
• For both vertical and horizontal splits, the image is processed from top left to bottom right.

THE

CUCKOLD's

CHRONICLE:

BEING

SELECT TRIALS

FOR

| ADULTRY. INCEST, | IMBECILITY, RAVISHMENT, &c. |

VOLUME I

BOSTON:

PRINTED FOR THOSE WHO CHOOSE TO PURCHASE.

1798

C9634c

PREFACE.

AT a period like this, when the great mass of the people appears entirely devoted to Political pursuits; when ancient prejudices, or Utopian plans, actuate the views and engross the attention of all, and schemes of supporting or reforming our system of Government, supply a thousand requisites to fill up the blank spaces in the minds of men; but to which requisites there are so many objections; a publication which should attempt a part in divesting the general pursuit of subjects, so petulant and inflammatory, might neither be unnecessary nor unacceptable. A Chronicle like this, seems long to have been wanting to concenter in one point of view, the scenes of wickedness and criminality, of brutality and lust, of farcical absurdities, and ridiculous propensity, which have, during the course of later years, so strangely attracted the notice of the Public, and demanded the interposition of the law: various publications have, indeed, given many details of these important circumstances to the world, but every one in such a mode as to be liable to the greatest objection. The form of Deposition, is the way in which every Trial, however uninteresting, has been given, a mode which the fanciful scenes of the most amusing subject could hardly enliven, but which must be peculiarly cold and repulsive, when employed as the vehicle of facts neither extraordinary nor important. The minutest occurrences, so circumstantially repeated, the same ground so frequently traversed, and the perpetual recurrence of the dull stile of legal procedure, form objections invincible against the imperfect collection we at present possess of Trials for the violation of the Hymeneal vow. The largest collection we have at present, is totally inadequate to a full comprehension of the subject, as it comprises at most only the course of twenty years, viz. from 1760, to 1780. The inexhaustible fund of interesting matter contained in the State Trials, the striking occurences of various Courts of Jurisdiction, and the vast number of Trials, since the year 1780, which exist only in a fugitive state, call loudly for a completer mode of collection, than has as yet been attempted. Our grand object will be to present to the Public, a series of circumstances of such mingled seriousness and absurdity, such criminal turpitude and such ridiculous weakness, comprising scenes so wildly ridiculous, and so extravagantly absurd, as must arrest every attention, and furnish food for every disposition, and this we shall convey in the easy mode of *Narrative*, by which we shall simplify the most intricate occurrences, and obviate that complaint of dulness and langour, which has so long and so justly been urged against these compositions. That neighbouring nation, which led the way to polished grace, and obsequious gallantry in modern Europe, which established the science of superior breeding, and matured the refined eloquence of Courts, introduced, with her fascinating influence, the contempt of those ties of connubial love which are really so sacred, and, before she uttered her political metaphysics, contaminated private life by the less laboured doctrines of her accomplished men of fashion and courtiers. Royalty and elegance seem to have yielded, in that country, to the stern virtues of haughty Republicanism, and England possesses devotees of pleasure, seemingly resolved to wear the glaring laurel of profligate fame, which France has resigned. You know it, (meaning the dishonour of your bed) said a celebrated French moralist and wit, it is but a trifle, if you are ignorant of it, it is nothing. We seem, in many instances, to have improved on this consolatory axiom, to have considered the knowledge, nay, it might be nearly said, the damning sight of our most infamous dishonour as nothing. Of this the stores of novel information, we have to bring forwards will afford decisive proof, and the whole arrangement of curious matter, furnishes heroines amongst the ladies, not unworthy of being ranked with an Errington or a Newton, though as yet wanting their fame and characters among the Gentlemen deserving of being ranked in the highest class of seducers, although capricious fortune has denied them their well earned celebrity.

To the youthful, the gay, and the fashionable, the scenes of frolic and amusement, of subterfuge and intrigue, of art and of temptation, now intended to be laid before them, will supply an inexhauftible fund of amufement, and afford a fpecies of relaxation, conveying more inftruction for the ufe of domeftic life, than the moft auftere dogma of morality can offer. To men of a ferious and contemplative turn, this Work will not be without its ufe; the leffons of morality we fhall occafionaly interfperfe, will, in concert with their own reflections, fupply a fund of argument highly gratifying to philofophical minds, if there are perfons who affert that we have nearly run the career of human affairs, that we have trod over the fteps of Rome, Athens and Sparta, and attained the climax of national depravity, to fuch men it will furely appear highly neceffary, to exhibit the aggregate view of what lengths we have gone in the commiffion of crimes, which, by ftriking at the root of domeftic felicity, endangers the whole religion and moral character of the State. From fuch men, we naturally muft expect the warmeft patronage, and confider their approbation of our plan, as the beft evidence of the warmth they feel for the welfare of their country.

THE

CUCKOLD's CHRONILCE.

The Trial between the Right Hon. Sir Richard Worfley, Bart. and George Maurice Biffett, Efq. Defendant, for Criminal Converfation with the Plaintiff's Wife, on Thurfday 21ft of Feb. 1782,

THIS Trial, not more celebrated in the annals of gallantry, than in the records of judicial proceeding; quoted alike by the gay amateurs of diffipated pleafure, and the fedulous inveftigator of legal bufinefs, we have chofen for the opening of thefe interefting Memoirs. The volatile indifference of this modern Meffalina, the defpicable meannefs of her wretched Hufband, and the evidence of her Gallants, now directly pointed. and now curioufly evafive, furnifh a fource of fuch mingled amufement and inftruction, as few inftances poffefs the power of furpaffing. or indeed of equalling.

This caufe was tried before the Right Honourable William, Earl of Mansheld, and a Special Jury.

For the Plaintiff, the Counfel were,

Mr. Attorney General,   Mr. Lee,
Mr Dunning,   Mr. Erfkine.

For the Defendant,

Mr Bearcroft,   Mr. Howorth.
Mr. Pechell,

The Declaration ftated, that the defendant, on the 19th of November, 1781, and at other times between that day and the 24th of the fame month, at Weftminfter, in the county of Middlefex; with force and arms, made an affault on Seymour, the wife of the plaintiff, and then and there debauched, deflowered, lay with and carnally was connected with her, the faid Seymour, to the plaintiff s damage of 20,000l.

To this declaration the defendant pleaded not guilty, and thereupon iffue was joined.

The caufe was opened by Mr. Attorney General, who ftated, that the plaintiff lived at Apuldurcomb, in the Ifle of Wight, and was worth about 5000l. a year, that Lady Worfley was the daughter of Sir John Fleming, and that Sir Richard had a fortune of about 70,000l. or more with her: the plaintiff and fhe were married on the 15th of September 1775, and had iffue two children, a fon and a daughter, that the defendant was an officer in the Hampfhire Militia, of which the plaintiff was Colonel, and that their acquaintance had been only from the end of February, or commencement of March, 1781, and that it originated in confequence of a burgage tenure Mr Biffet poffeffed in the Ifle of Wight, and which, added to an eftate of 800l a year in Somerfetfhire. made his income about 1500l a year, this burgage-tenure, Sir Richard, impelled by parliamentary motives, wifhed to purchafe: this occafioned their firft meeting, and foon afterwards Sir Richard gave Mr. Biffet a commiffion in his regiment.   That the greateft intimacy now took place between them . the plaintiff had a houfe at Maidftone, and the defendant, while at camp in Coxheath, regularly visited him there. That after the breaking up of the camp, they came to Lewes, where Sir Richard had a house, and Mr. Bissett lodgings, and the greatest friendship subsisted between them, till that unhappy event, the groundwork of this action, took place.

After this opening, the evidence for the plaintiff was brought forwards. The marriage of the 15th of September 1775, was admitted Captain Leverage, an officer in the Hampshire Militia, and an acquaintance and neighbour of Sir Richard's, declared, that he had no knowledge of Captain Bissett, previous to his seeing him on the parade at High Wickham, after his receiving his commission from Sir Richard, that he recollected Sir Richard Worsley and Captain Bissett's being at Cox heath together, and that there seemed to be the greatest intimacy between Sir Richard and his family, and him, Mr. Bissett, Captain Leverage said, seemed to him a man of fashion, and extensive intimacy with the brighter circle of society At the breaking up of the camp, he came with Sir Richard's family to Lewes, and visited also at Maidstone. Mr. Bissett had lodgings at Lewes, and was frequently at Sir Richard's house there On Sunday the 18th of November, Lady Worsley drank tea and supped at the house of Captain Leverage, at Lewes, on the invitation of the Captain and his family, Captain Bissett came with her. Sir Richard Worsley did not come in pursuance of the invitation, but about ten o'clock in the evening, sent an apology by Captain Worsley, that he was not well and wished to be excused, that he could not attend that evening, and was then taking some sack whey for his indisposition.

This invitation to Captain Leverage's house was general married ladies, as well as their husbands, being invited. Lady Worsley came about seven o'clock in the evening. This friendly assembly, Lady Worsley was the first who attempted to break up she intimated a desire to part between twelve and one o'clock. Mrs Leverage was apprehensive, that the company was not perfectly agreeable to her, by her eagerness to go, and wished

her not to urge her departure; Lady Worfley fat down
again, and Captain Biffett looking at his watch, and ad-
dreffing himfelf to her Lady fhip, faid, Don't go yet, upon this fhe ftaid till a quarter paft one.

On their departure, Captain Leverfage took a light,
intending to accompany them home, Sir Richard's houfe
being nearly oppofite, he went within a few yards of the
door, when Captain Biffett begged he would not give
himfelf any further trouble, on this, Captain Leverfage
wifhing them a good night, returned home. About four
or five o clock in the morning, he was awaked by a vio-
ent rapping at his door· he arofe directly, and going to
the window, found it was one of Sir Richard's fervants,
who brought his mafter's compliments, and a polite meffage, defiring Lady Worfley would come home; the
Captain told him Lady Worfley had been gone ever
fince one o clock in about ten minutes or a quarter of
an hour, Sir Richard himfelf appears, Leverfage, fays he
where is Lady Worfley?

When Captain Leverfage came to this occurrence,
the Attorney-General, actuated, no doubt by a laudable
zeal for his client's intereft, ftopt him, and after afking
one or two queftions not very material, left him to the
crofs-examination of Mr. Bearcroft, from which as little
remarkable occurred.

A Mr Sadler proved the hand writing of Captain Biffett, in two letters, the firft evinced the friendly intercourfe which fubfifted between the plaintiff and the defendant, it congratulated Sir Richard on his Lady's happy delivery of a daughter, and expreffed the writer's
great anxiety for Lady Worflev's health, and his earneft
defire for her return to quarters the fecond letter was
wrote the morning of the elopement, inclofed the Captain s commiffion, which Sir Richard was defired to accept, and named Lord Deerhurft s Cleaveland Row, as
the place where an anfwer would be expected.

Francis Godfrey, a fervant of Sir Richard Worfley's
remembered Lady Worfley's going to Captain Leverfage s, fhe told him at going out, that if any body called

for her, fhe fhould not fup at home that evening : he fat
up for her till between five and fix o'clock in the morning, about five Sir Richard called him, and fent him to
Captain Leverfage's, Sir Richard, he faid, appeared to be
much difturbed; after repeated enquiries after Lady
Worfley, he was told that fhe had left Captain Leverfage's at one in the morning, accompanied by Captain
Biffett. This man had only lived with Sir Richard one
day.

Mr. Stubbs, the landlord of the houfe where Captain
Biffett lodged, did not remember his coming home on
this memorable morning, but between three and four, the
Captain knocked at his chamber door, and begged to
light a candle, in this he was accommodated. he was then
in his bed-gown, and directly returned to his room, in a
fhort time he came out of his room and called the fervant,
Conolly, and begged him to go down ftairs, in a little
time he called the man again, and then the man or fome
other perfon went out of the door, in about ten minutes
the fafh was thrown up. Mr Stubbs got out of bed to
know if the Captain wanted any thing, but was anfwered
in the negative foon after the perfon, whoever it was,
came in again, and juft afterwards a chaife arrived at the
door. it did not, however, ftop, but went on to turn about,
and fome time after, the Captain and fome other perfon
went down ftairs, and the chaife drove off

Mr. Attorney-General queftioned what the time might
be, but Lord Mansfield remarked, ' this is nothing but
travelling a long way about, why don't you come to the
point and bring them to London at once?'

T. Bourn, the waiter at the Royal Hotel, in Pall Mall,
remembered a Lady and gentleman coming there about
two in the morning, of the 19th of November, he went
to the chaife door, and the Gentleman let the window
down about half way; on his attempting to open the door,
the gentleman pulled it up again. he ftopped a fhort time,
a¡d the window was let down half way again, and as he
was opening the door, the window was once more thrown
up. Mr Wefton then came to the door, and the Gen-

tleman and lady ftepped out, they entered the houfe very
quickly, and was fhewn up ftairs into a room named the
Apollo, a large drawing-room, and they then ordered
breakfaft directly. The waiter carried breakfaft up ftairs
and prepared a bed for them as near the dining-room as
he poffibly could, and then, faid he, they went to bed.

Lord Mansfield afked, how he knew they went to bed:
the waiter's reafon for thinking fo was, that he went to
take the things away, and they had left the dining-room.
His Lordfhip again afked, if he faw them go into the
bed-room; to which he was anfwered, no · what induced
the waiter to think they lay together in one bed, he
declared, was the plain reafon that there was no other
bed in the room they ftaid at the Hotel four or five
days, and during that time paffed for man and wife, not
that they faid any thing importing that they were fo, but,
knowing no otherwife, he fuppofed that to be the cafe.

Ann Watkinfon, the houfe-keeper at the Royal Hotel,
knew that the Lady and Gentleman, relative to whom
the waiter had fworn, lodged in that houfe, that their
dining-room was called the Apollo, and their bed-chamber No 14. She was ordered to prepare the bed-room
and accordingly did. fhe never faw them in bed, but fhe
imagined they were, as it was prepared for them, and
fhe alfo heard them fpeak in bed: fhe faw the bed afterward, and was convinced that fome perfon had lain in it.
She never heard any converfation between them, and
did not know who they were when they came into the
houfe, but had been informed fince. when fhe once went
into the room there was a lady there, and fhe afked Lady
Worfley her name, and fhe anfwered that her name was
Worfley

Mrs Commande, who lived at the Royal Hotel, recollected a Lady and Gentleman coming there, on the
19th Novem and remaining there till the 24th fhe did not
then know them, but had fince been acquainted that their
names were Lady Worfley and Captain Biffet: they did
not affume any name while they remained there nor
was fhe able to obferve any thing in their behaviour,

which could empower her to judge of the form of their connexion. On the morning they went away, (the 24th) Lady Worfley's name was mentioned, the occafion was, Mrs. Commande introducing two of Sir Richard's fervants, a woman and a groom, to Lady Worfley and Mr Biffett, while they were in bed, fhortly afterwards, Captain Biffett fent for her into the dining-room, defired to know her motives for fhewing fuch perfons into Lady Worfley's bed-room. and faid, fuch behaviour to ladies of quality would not benefit their houfe, it was about one o'clock in the morning Mrs Commande faid, when fhe faw Lady Worfley and Captain Biffet in bed together.

A Mr Herne only faid, that he was the receiver of Mr. Biffett's rents, the amount of which were 800l. or fomewhat better than 800l a year.

This was the whole of the evidence adduced for the plaintiff, feveral particulars of it, perhaps, afford fcope for remark to the curious obferver. How aufpicious was the commencement of the Friendfhip between Sir Richard and the Captain! he difcovered, no doubt, fome kindred virtue in the breaft of Mr. Biffett, which attached him by the moft congenial fympathy. With the view of having fo valued a friend near him, he offers him a commiffion in that part of the Hampfhire Militia, which he himfelf commands, yet luckier, the Captain entertains as high a regard for *Lady* Worfley as for his friend, doubtlefs, at firft, a very pure attachment! but then comes this unfortunate invitation to a friend's houfe, and ftill more unfortunately at this very crifis, poor Sir Richard finds himfelf indifpofed, and is neceffitated to remain at home, nurfing himfelf with fack whey, whilft the fcheme of his blackeft difhonour is planning, his wife and her lover, tempted by the opportunity, at once forfeit all their claims to virtue, and elope the romantic attachment of the friends, is in a moment diffolved. Sir Richard, with a patience truly exemplary, waits till five in the morning, and then fends his man to beg his Lady to return home, he comes back with the doleful intelligence, that fhe has

left the houfe where fhe fupped, fome hours, in company
with her guardian Captain   Sir Richard is ftark raving
mad at this news, and immediately repairs to his friend's
houfe, after alarming the whole neighbourhood, he can
gain no better tidings · but here the prudence of his counfel, the Attorney-General, interrupted Captain Leverfage's evidence, and prevented our hearing thofe effecting
burfts of tender anxiety, which muft have placed Sir Richard's character in the moft amiable point of view ; however, let us in pity hope, that the fituation of his mind was
not fo cruelly agonizing, as to have rendered Shakefpear's
lines applicable to him.

‘ Not Poppy, nor Mandragora, nor all the drowfy Syrups of the
Eaft,
‘Shall medicine thee, to that fweet fleep, which thou had'ft yefter-
night.’

We will rather fuppofe that another potion of that fack
whey which unqueftionably fupported him during the
abfence of Lady Worfley, reftored tranquility to his agitated mind, we cannot even imagine, that his refentment
was fo bitter, as to induce him to order his fervants to
penetrate the room where there Lady flept, and thereby
give occafion to thofe pathetic remonftrances, which his
friend Captain B. was obliged to make ufe of to the offi-
cious waiting-woman, who fo impertinently intruded them
into the prefence of *a lady of quality.*

The evidence for the defendant now came forwards;
and Mr Bearcroft, in anfwer to this evidence, did not attempt to make any defence in controvertion of the charge
exhibited againft the defendant, but was very ready to
admit, that the plaintiff was entitled to a verdict.   The
only queftion which then remained was upon the fubject
of damages, in mitigation of which only he would defend his client; and did not doubt to prove, to the fatif-
faction of the jury, that Sir Richard not only acquiefced
under repeated acts of his own difhonour with various
perfons, but even excited and encouraged it: on which—
Lord Mansfield faid, if a plaintiff encourages, or is pri-

ty to, or confenting at all. or contributing to the debauch
ery of his wife, or joins in it, he ought not to recover a
verdict.

Mr. Bearcroft then ftated, that he could not only prove
this to be the fact, but that he fhould prove by the affidavits of the woman who attended the bath at Maidftone, that the plaintiff there had abfolutely raifed the defendant upon his fhoulders, to view his naked wife while
bathing, and at the fame time called to her, faying, Seymour! Seymour! *Bifett is looking at you!* and that fhe,
on coming out after fhe had dreffed herfelf, joined the
Gentlemen; and they all went off together in a hearty
laugh at the tranfaction which had paffed. The bathing-
woman was ill, and could not attend the trial herfelf to
give evidence of this fact, but that it had been agreed between the parties, that the attornies on each fide fhould
go down to the place for the purpofe of taking the affidavits, and in order to view the fituation, which they had
done, and which affidavits would be read.

That the defendant could not poffibly be the father of
the child born in Auguft laft, as his firft acquaintance
with the plaintiff commenced only in March, fo that he
had not baftardized the plaintiff's iffue.

He wondered why they had not called fome perfons
belonging to, or about the family, in order to prove how
the parties lived together; a circumftance very material
in a cafe like this they had only called one perfon belonging to the family; and that was the butler, who had
lived in the houfe but one day, and who, of courfe, could
not fpeak to that point.

That the licentious conduct of Lady Worfley, was fo
notorious, that it had been the fubject of common converfation, and that many Ladies of diftinction, in the Ifle
of Wight and elfwhere, had frequently remonftrated
with Sir Richard on that fubject, and told him, that if he
did not attempt to reftrain her conduct, her character
would be ruined and deftroyed, that the anfwer Sir Richard made was, that Lady Worfley liked it, and he chofe
to do it to oblige her, upon which a very fenfible Lady.

who had frequently remonstrated with him on the subject, replied, " If this is the case, God help you ! you are the " most contented—Husband I ever knew:" and that, from the Lady's many prior connections, the idea of seduction by the present defendant was totally done away.

Evidence for the Defendant.

Mary Mariott being unable to attend the trial, the following affidavits were read.

Mary Mariott deposed, that Lady Worsley used to come to the cold bath, near Maidstone, to bathe, and that she used to attend her, that Sir Richard and Mr. Bissett were generally with her; and that the last time she came, which was about noon, in September last, and at the latter end of the hop-season, Sir Richard Worsley and Mr Bissett staid at the door without, while she bathed, that after she had bathed, she retired into a corner to put on her shift, as Ladies usually do after bathing, and then returned to dress herself, and sat herself down on the seat. that there is a window over the door of the building in which the bath is, and which is the only inlet for light into the bath, and from which any person, who is sitting down on the seat, may be seen, but not when retired into the corner; that when she had almost finished dressing herself, Sir Richard tapped at the door, and said, " Seymour ! Seymour ! Bissett is going to get up to look at you,' or words to that effect, and, looking round, she saw his face at the window, that he continued there about five minuets; that she did not see the plaintiff on the outside, but believes he must help the defendant up; and that after Lady Worsley had dressed herself, she went out, and they were all mery and laughing together· that, excepting this, she never saw any improper conduct or behaviour in the said three persons, unless what is above stated may be thought so.

In addition to this, there was another affidavit read, in which she *believed* that Mr. Bissett could *not* have got up to the window, unless he had been assisted by Sir

Richard, or stood upon his shoulders; and that Sir Richard might easily have pulled him down if he pleased.

The Right Honourable Lord Deerhurst said, that he was first acquainted with Lady Worsley, in the year 1779 he esteemed her conduct as very dissolute, and thought that conjugal fidelity was not one of her virtues he was intimate with Sir Richard, but never witnessed any exertions made by him, to check the lewd depravity of her life. His Lordship being on a visit at Sir Richard's house, in the Isle of Wight, Sir Richard seeing Lady Worsley pass by the window, said to Lord Deerhurst, that many young men had assailed her virtue. but that all had proved unsuccessful, and that he gave him full liberty to attempt her chastity, this his Lordship considered as the effect of a light and airy manner, and this Lord Mansfield said, went for nothing. Lord Deerhurst continued at Sir Richard's house ten days, during that time, Sir Richard once found him in the dressing-room adjacent to her Ladyship's bed-chamber, at four o'clock in the morning Sir Richard pretended amazement at finding him there, and exclaimed, Deerhurst, how came you here? after that his Lordship retired to his bed-chamber, he was, however, suffered to attend Lady Worsley, as if no remarkable occurrence had taken place he attended her to Southampton, at Kingston and Godalmin, at all these places alone, and with the knowledge of Sir Richard. At Kingston and Godalmin, Lord Deerhurst met her by appointment. Mr. Howarth, one of the defendant's counsel, asked his Lordship, if he was criminally connected with Lady Worsley at the last-mentioned place; but his Lordship claimed the protection of the Judge, and Lord Mansfield decided, that it was a question he had no right to answer. On the cross examination of Mr Attorney-General, Lord Deerhurst denied any particular permission from Sir Richard to attend Lady Worsley, and said, that other Gentlemen attended her Ladyship, without objection from Sir Richard His Lordship acknowledged carrying a message from Sir Richard to Lady

B

Worfley at the Hotel, and receiving for anfwer, that he might inform Sir Richard, that it was in vain for him to attempt the recovery of Lady Worfley, as fhe was determined never to unite with him again.

The acquaintance of Lord Peterborough with Lady Worfley, commenced nearly about the opening of Ranelagh, in the year 1780· he was firft introduced to her at Sadler's Wells, by Lord Deerhurft, he had not any intimacy with Sir Richard, either then or afterwards, nor even fpoke to him during his acquaintance with Lady Worfley: he made no remarks on the behaviour of Sir Richard and his Lady, as he never faw them together, but did not think her conduct quite confiftent with the character of a decent and virtuous married woman

Bouchier Smith, Efq was acquainted with Lady Worfley, in the year 1779; he thought fhe betrayed a great difregard of character. he was in company with Lady Worfley, on a party at Shooter's Hill, when they met Sir Richard in a phæton, and her Ladyfhip many times afked him to accompany them, but he refufed, and fet off for town; he did not remark any thing elfe particular that day.

The Marquis of Graham's acquaintance with Lady Worfley, begun four years prior to the trial, he had no intimacy with Sir Richard. he fometimes vifited at his houfe, but not frequently. Lady Worfley was gay, free, and airy, in a manner he thought carried rather too far for a married woman, he did not obferve any abfolute impropriety or immodefty in her conduct, as far as it refpected converfation to a queftion which nearly related to himfelf, the Marquis refufed to anfwer

A Mr. Clark gave an account of the firft interview between Sir Richard Worfley and Mr. Biffett, and the occafion of it

The Honourable Charles Wyndham's acquaintance with Lady Worfley, commenced between three and four years before the trial. he was not acquainted with Sir Richard at that time, and fince his intimacy has been very flight. he never thought the conduct of Lady Worfley becoming; he remembered Lady Worfley's prefent-ing him with a gold-ring in Kenfington Gardens.

Doctor Ofborn remembered Lady Worfley about Au-guft, in the year 1780, at Sir Richard's houfe in town: being queftioned as to the condition he found her in, he replied, ' Between a patient and a phyfician, there is an implied fecrecy, the nature of the cafe required it, and that being the ftate of the cafe I fhould hardly conceive myfelf at liberty to declare it, but I have the Lady's per-miffion to give the truth. he faid, he was not employed by Sir Richard being again queftioned as to the fitua-tion in which he found her, he replied, ' I believe it was never known, at leaft I never was afked my opinion of the diforder; nor did I think it neceffary to mention it, my bufinefs was to cure her; and I do not chufe to talk upon the fubject, one way or other ' Upon this anfwer, Lord Mansfield remarked, ' you might have told them when they firft interrogated you, that you wifhed to be excufed.'

Here the evidence for the defendant clofed. Mr. J. Farrer, the plaintiff's attorney, was brought forwards and fworn on his behalf he faid, he went down to the cold bath mentioned in the affidavit, he faw the place on which Mr Biffett got to look into the bath, and believed that he might mount it with a great deal of eafe, and without the help of Sir Richard, it was about breaft high; there was an arm chair placed on the outfide, and when he was on the chair, he faid, he could raife himfelf to the window with great facility the window was about four feet high, and the feat on the outfide of the bath.

Mr. Attorney-General made a fhort reply on the fub-ject of damages.

LORD MANSFIELD.

Gentlemen of the Jury,

There arifes upon this evidence a ferious queftion for your confideration —The nature of the action is fuch, that the defendant cannot confefs a verdict, becaufe this is between the Hufband and Wife and tho Adulterer, and further proceedings may be had, therefore, the verdict, you give muft be out of the truth and juftice of the cafe, and the juftice of the evidence.

Now, the fingle queftion is, Whether Sir Richard has not been privy to the proftitution of his wife? affenting to, and encouraging and exciting even this defendant? And, if he is fo, upon your opinion of the evidence, he ought *not* to recover in this action——if he is not, why then the only queftion that remains, is upon the fubject of damages; upon which I will not fay a word to you. You are the beft judges of that.

This woman, for three or four years, has been proftituted with a variety of people; that is extremely clear. A ftronger inftance than the Doctor's appearance this day, and what he has faid, need not have been brought. ——In the year 1779, Lord Deerhurft knew Lady Worfley; fhe was very profligate, and no ftep was taken by Sir Richard to prevent her. he continued in the ifle of Wight ten days. and he has mentioned a converfation that paffed between them and Sir Richard, which ought to be laid out of the cafe, becaufe it feems to be ironical : " That many young men had tried her, without fuccefs; and that he might take his chance with her " But he fays, once the plaintiff found him in Lady Worfley's dreffing-room at four o clock in the morning ; and he only fays to him, " Deerhurft, how came you here?" And there is no further explanation or examination between them. Is it not extraordinary to find a Gentleman in his Lady's dreffing room at four o'clock in the morning, and nothing further faid? All is well, they are all good company the next morning, and fome few days afterwards, Lady Worfley is going to Southampton At the fame time Sir Richard goes eight miles with her, and leaves Lord Deerhurft to go on with her to Southampton : he goes on with her to Southampton, he ftays there twenty-four hours, and fhe ftays three or four days —*yet there is no appearance of jealoufy in the Hufband!* This evidence deferves your confideration.

Another piece of evidence is, that of the woman at the bath at Maidstone; she swears, she *believes* it was impossible for Mr Bisset to have got up the height of the balcony, to look into the bath, unless he had stood upon Sir Richard's shoulders. but this is matter of belief; and they have called the Attorney, and you have heard his evidence, he went down there to take the affidavits: he says he got up with a great deal of ease, and without assistance, that he got up first on an arm-chair which stood on the outside of the bath, and then it was only four feet above him, so that, if he had not stood upon Sir Richard's shoulders, he might easily have pulled him down if he pleased, instead of which, he only taps at the door, and says Seymore! Seymore! *Bissett is looking at you.* And when she is dressed and comes out, she joins them, and they are all jolly and merry, and laughing, and so away together

This is the evidence which they have given, and if upon that evidence you think the Husband was privy to consenting, and encouraging this debauchery, he ought not to have your verdict, but if you think he is entitled to your verdict, then the only point for your consideration is, What damages you will give——You will confider of your verdict. and give what damages you think proper.

The Jury went out of court, and after debating near an hour, returned with a verdict for the plaintiff, giving him *only One Shilling* damages.

The whole of the evidence for the defendant, is not less curious than the testimony brought forwards in favour of the plaintiff the remark made by the Lady, who had so frequently advised Sir Richard on the conduct of his Wife, must have been peculiarly grateful to a man of his refined and delicate sentiments, when his amiable good nature prevented him from repressing those irregularities of Lady Worsley's conduct, which their mutual friends apprehended, might terminate so disagreeably, the kind compliment of his being the most *contented*——Husband the Lady ever knew, must have been particularly consoling· and the word Husband so kindly substituted for that of

Cuckold! but how was this poor Gentleman deluded
through the whole of the bufinefs? relying on that virtue,
he had intuitively difcovered in the bofom of Captain
Biffett, he with the moft unaffected fimplicity, and fuperiority to mean fufpicion, affifted that Gentleman in taking a furvey of Lady Worfley's charms, when uncovered
in the bath.   And yet perhaps, this was the firft temptation
which fhook his friend's virtue, though none of the parties
betrayed any fymptoms of apprehenfion, that any thing
wrong had happened, but retired laughing, joking, completely merry, happy, and wife.

Sir Richard's conduct, with refpect to Lord Deerhurft,
was not lefs expreffive of confidence in his wife and
here the obfervation muft ftrike us, of that general want
of acquaintance with Sir Richard, which moft of the
young men of fashion who appeared on the Trial profeffed though fo friendly with his Lady, they knew but
little of him, doubtlefs, the elevation of Sir Richard's
integrity, and the refined purity of his fentiments, were
circumftances but little congenial to the purfuits and attachments of thofe characters, their particular referve,
however, as to betraying any circumftances which might
have affected the Lady's honour, may be urged as an
exception in favour of their nicety what could be a greater inftance of Sir Richard's purity, than his obliging permiffion to Lord Deerhurft, to affail the virtue of Lady
Worfley, or the good natured manner in which he paffed
over the extraordinary circumftance of his being fo near
her bed-chamber, at four o'clock in the morning! This
could have arofe from nothing but the confcious virtue
of Sir Richard's own immaculate bofom, and how muft
we commiferate, that fo amiable a man fhould fuffer by
fraud and deception!

To have feen things in the light Sir Richard did, he
doubtlefs muft have poffeffed a different kind of vifion
from that of perfons in general: perhaps a fomewhat refembled the ' poetical fecond fight' of Puff in the Critic,
when the diftracted heroine of the Poet's Tragedy, is raving, in all the agonies of defpair, for the lofs of her lover,

the infpiration of the Mufes pourtrays the Spanifh Fleet in the livelieft colours to her difturbed mind, but her father, who, to ufe the language of Puff's friend, 'makes an allowance for this poetical fecond fight,' declares, that the 'Spanifh fleet fhe cannot fee, becaufe 'tis not in fight.' The character of this father is reprefented by the Author, as that of a 'plain matter of fact man,' exactly this 'plain matter of fact man,' was Lord Mansfield. cafting wide the poetic fiction, a fancied fecond fight, or whatever mode of refined illufion Sir Richard might be impelled by, he appealed only to well attefted and corroborated circumftances, and directing the Jury by irrefiftible argument, left to the Baronet the fad recompence afforded him by the verdict

What the feelings of Sir Richard were, when he heard the determination, it would not be very eafy to imagine the contemptuous pity of his friends, the indignation of the Public, and the fentiments of his own mind, muft have afforded a happy combination the impartial Public did not hefitate in giving their judgment, and all pofterity who may hear of the curious difcuffion, will find no difficulty in delivering an adequate decifion.

Remarkable Indictment, extracted from
No. 4254, of the St. James's Evening
Post, published April 7th, 1787,

AT Leicester assizes no persons were capitally con-
victed, and but two burnt in the hand. and four transport-
ed, an odd Trial came on, the case being thus.
One Baggerly, being hired to work about five miles
from Grooby. and being jealous of his wife, was afraid to
leave her to her own inclinations, therefore put in execution a most villainous and barbarous design, which the
wife told her mother and sisters of, and they in the neighbourhood, who released the woman from her great pain,
and took him up, and at the last assizes he was indicted,
which indictment was as follows :
" *Leicestershire. ss.* The Jurors of our sovereign
" Lord the King, upon their oaths present, that George
" Baggerly. late of Grooby, labourer, on the 15th day
" of October, in the tenth year of our sovereign Lord the
" King, with force and arms, at Grooby, against the peace
" of our said Lord the King, then and there did make
" an assault; and that the said George Baggerly, put a
" certain needle and thread into and through the skin and
" flesh of the private parts of the said Dorothy, in di-
" vers places, then and there wickedly, barbarously and
" inhumanly did force, and the said private parts of her
" the said Dorothy Baggerly, with the needle and thread
" aforesaid, did then and there sew up to the great dam-
" age of the said Dorothy, and against the peace of our
" sovereign Lord the King. his Crown and dignity "
To which indictment the prisoner pleaded Guilty, and
the Court gave him a very severe reprimand, but con-
sidering his great poverty, fined him Twenty Shillings,

and to be imprifoned for two years, and to find fecuri-
ty for his good behaviour for feven years.

As he was carrying from his Trial to the jail, the women fell upon him, and fcratched him terribly, calling
him all the ill names they could think of, &c.

This very fingular expedient to efcape Cuckoldom,
added to many other inftances which have occurred, is
a ftriking proof that Jealoufy will impel mankind to the
commiffion of more atrocious acts, than any other paffion.

The Trial of the Rev. Mr. James Al-tham, of Harlow, in the County of Effex, for Adultery, Defamation, and Obfcenity; in the Confiftorial and E-pifcopal Court of London, at Doc-tor's Commons.   1785.

WE have hardly any need to premife, that the whole
of this trial, is a ftriking picture of a feries of excentrici-
ties that have fcarcely an equal in the annals of extrava-
gance.   To defcribe, or even to attempt to fet them off
in any other way, than exhibiting them developed of legal jargon, is beyond our plan.   The libel gives them
in an outline ftriking indeed.   We fhall firft give this as
it ftands, and afterwards, the particulars of the evidence.

The firft fpecifies, that the Rev. James Altham was
legally married to Sufannah Parkhurft, now Sufannah
Altham, and that they have lived and cohabited together,
as lawful hufband and wife. That, notwithftanding fuch
marriage, the Rev. James Altham gave a letter to Ann

Saunders, addreffed to her, defiring her to read it at her leifure, and that fuch letter contained many ftrong expreffions of love and regard; and mentioned, if James Altham was to die, he would leave her two hundred pounds; and that, if his wife died, he would marry her, if he had not a quarter of an hour to live.

II. That the fum of fixty pounds was afterwards paid by the faid Rev. James Altham, that fuch letter might be cancelled, and all converfation relating thereto, fuppreffed as foon as poffible,

III. That the Rev. James Altham appointed to meet Ann Saunders in a place called the Shrubbery, and that fhe met him accordingly, and that then and there the Rev. James Altham, and Ann Saunders, committed the crime of adultery together, and that, on another day, James Altham prevailed on Ann Saunders to lie with him, in the entry or paffage of the houfe inhabited by Mr. John Edwards.

IV. James Altham is charged with having confeffed that he had twice lain with the faid Ann Saunders, and thereby committed the crime of adultery with her.

V. That he is vicar of St. Olave Jewry, and rector of St. Martin, Ironmonger-lane.

VI. That, fpeaking of his amours in public company, affirmed that Mrs. Elizabeth Wenham had kiffed and fmacked him, and called him "her dear Jemmy," that he fpoke very indecently of the faid Mrs. Elizabeth Wenham; and intimated that her hafband, Mr. John Wenham, was not a fufficient man for her, and that Mrs Wenham wanted him, the faid James Altham, to lie with her

VII. That he had faid that he was of a very warm conftitution, and that he had been concerned with fifty women in the parifh of Harlow, in Effex, and, as a proof of the warmth of his conftitution, that he went home and laid with his wife immediately after lying with Ann Saunders in the Shrubbery.

VIII That he had faid he kept a girl whilft he was at college, and mentioned how he fupported her. That he was very unguarded in his converfation, and frequently expreffed him in obfcene and indecent terms, fuch as were highly improper for a clergyman to make ufe of.

IX. That he frequently importuned Ann Tavner to be criminally acquainted with him; and tried his utmoft to prevail on her to confent to gratify his criminal inclinations, by promifing what a friend he would be to her. That after trying every method of perfuafion with her, he even attempted to force her; and once, in particular, he called upon her in the morning, and began putting his hand in her bofom, and then tried to put his hand up her petticoats, and unbuttoned his breeches; and, if fhe had not refifted to her utmoft, fhe verily believes he would have carnally known her, and thereby have committed the crime of adultery.

X. That he called on Sarah Smith, wife of James Smith, of Harlow, and endeavoured to prevail on her to take her fifter, Ann Saunders, from Mr. Edwards's, where fhe then lived as a fervant, becaufe Mr. Edwards was a fingle man, and that he then told Sarah Smith, that he loved Ann Saunders beyond any other woman; that he had been dying for her eight or nine months, and that was the reafon why he wifhed fhe would take her from Mr. Edwards's, that he had even fainted away when he had feen her, and that Mrs. Altham had told him fhe was fure he loved that girl, that he had made Ann Saunders fome prefents.

XI. The libel further fets forth, that Ann Saunders confeffed, that James Altham had once lain with her in the Shrubbery, behind Mr. Edwards's houfe, and another time in the entry or paffage of the faid houfe, &c.

Ann Saunders of Oakely, in Effex, who was aged feventeen years and upwards, faid, that fhe knew James Altham for fix years paft, by living fervant at Dr. Fifher's in Harlow, where Mr. Altham frequently vifited, and further verified his perfon as being a prieft in holy orders, and a married man.

She faid, it was about the latter end of 1778, when Mr. Altham firft began to take particular notice of her, by taking hold of her, and squeezing her hand, smiling upon her, and making use of very endearing expressions. And that a short time before Christmas in that year, he met her and one Elizabeth Purkis, as they were walking in the road; that he called her to him, and said he wanted to speak to her, and that going about nine or ten yards from Elizabeth Purkis, he asked her if she would accept of a pair of silver buckles, which she refused, saying, she did not want any, and that she would not accept them : they then parted.

About a fortnight after, it seems Mr. Altham came to her master's house, and put a pair of silver buckles in her hand, and immediately went into the parlour. On the Easter Sunday following, he gave her a pocket-book with a silver clasp, and a set of instruments.—In June following, he took many opportunities of frequenting her company and being alone with her, when he behaved with the utmost fondness and affection.—About this time, it seems he gave her a letter, and told her to read it at her leisure, and then either return it to him, or burn it. this letter contained many strong professions of love and regard for her; and particularly mentioned, that if Mrs. Altham was to die he would marry Ann Saunders, even if he had not a quarter of an hour to live.——Ann Saunders seemed well acquainted with Mr. Altham's hand writing.

This letter, it appears, being accidentally found in Ann Saunders's possession by her brother, the circumstance soon came to the ears of Mr. Altham, who employed some of her relatives, and a Mr. Lushington, to get it out of their hands, but as they could not obtain this letter by persuasion, Mr. Lushington, at length, paid sixty pounds on Mr. Altham's account, and it was then given up.—Yet so strong was the desire of this gentleman, for the enjoyment of the person of Ann Saunders, that the payment of this money by no means abated his ardour: on the contrary, according to her own testimony, she very soon after met him in the Shrubbery by appointment. The time being evening, and after dark, was perfectly congenial to the good man's designs; for, according to the young lady's own account, he there and then prevailed over her to lie with him—so that in the ftarched phrafe of the law, they had the carnal ufe and knowledge of each other's bodies; and thereby committed the foul crimes of fornication, adultery, and incontinence.

This occurred in the month of April, but about the latter end of May, Mr. Altham happening to find her alone in the houfe of Mr. Edwards, at Harlow, again prevailed upon her to lie with him in the entry or paffage of the houfe. It feems, that fhe propofed going up ftairs into a room, but the godly zeal of this good man was fo warm, that he infifted upon fulfilling the firft great command, " Increafe and multiply," in the paffage.

In the courfe of this renewed intimacy, it feems that Mr. Altham was frequently foliciting Ann Saunders, to come and live with him.—It is to be obferved, that this gentleman's friends fet up the plea of infanity, in excufe for his conduct, and if even this plea was valid, it muft be admitted, upon his telling Ann Edwards, that he would not mind murdering his wife and children, if fhe would come and live with him, or words to the very fame effect.

Some particulars, in this extraordinary trial, offer a variety of reflections to the philofophical obferver —Mr. Altham, appears to have been continually boafting to the women, of his prowefs in the feats of love, and the variety of his connections with the fex. Few, very few women indeed, cordially defpife a rake: Mr. Altham's fuccefs plainly proves it. while, lamentable to be told, any pretenfion to extraordinary virtue, or chaftity in the male fex, is univerfally defpifed —'Oh Lud' A fellow's chaftity,' fays an old lady in a drama, 'why, I never heard of fuch a thing in my life!'—Conformably to this maxim, it feems Mr. Altham had told Ann Saunders, that he could lie with Mrs. Seed, a married woman, whenever he chofe or with her fifter Elizabeth Seed, both of Harlow. Indeed, it does not feem that this gentleman thought of any thing fo much, as of increafing the lambs of his flock.

As we have treated of the letter, and the negociation in general terms, we fhall now come to its contents, and

the manner of its being discovered.   It seems, that Mr.
John Edwards, surgeon and man-midwife, of Harlow,
with whom Ann Saunders lived servant, being one day
in want of a pen and ink, he went into a room opposite
to her's, which was not used, where he saw several papers
lying upon a shelf, and among them a letter addressed,
" Dear Nanny !" he soon knew this to be Mr. Altham's
hand-writing, and as he directly conceived there had been
an intimacy between the parties, it also occurred to him,
how urgent Mr. Altham had been with Ann Saunders's
sister, to take her away from his house (Mr. Edwards's),
under the idea that he being a single man and living almost
alone, made it exceeding dangerous for a young woman
to stay with him '---Mr. Edwards as it is natural to suppose, immediately read the contents of this curious
Epistle ; and it is much to be regretted, that a copy of it
was not preserved. there is no doubt, that as it was got
out of the hands of the opposite party, for the consideration of sixty pounds, it was immediately and totally de-
stroyed.   It is certain, that it contained the following
verses :

> Dear maid, since thou hast charm'd my sight,
> Oh let my arms thy neck infold ,
> Those breasts so fair, those eyes so bright,
> What joy, what pleasure to behold !

The young woman to whom this was addressed, it
seems, was soon sensible of the danger of this precious e-
pistle, as Mr. Edwards had hardly come out of the apartment, when he met her coming in with great haste ; he informed her that he knew what she was in such haste about,
but that he had got the letter in his pocket, and was determined to shew it to her sister.   She then pressed him
very hard to deliver it up to her, but as he peremptorily
refused it, she began crying; but this was to no purpose.

So far from this indulgence, Mr. Edwards happening
to see Mr. Smith and his wife, the brother and sister of
Ann Saunders, that day, he read the contents of it to them
but did not give them the letter   It is commonly said,
that a woman cannot keep a secret ; but from this and a

thousand other instances, it is highly probable, that that proverb is equally applicable to the men.

The next day it seems, Mr. Edwards met Mr Altham in the fields, and after walking together some time, he introduced the affair of Ann Saunders, at least so much of it as had then got abroad in reply to which, Mr. Altham readily confessed that he had lain with her, but was very reluctant in acknowledging the letter in question. He indeed confessed, that he had written to her, but intirely declined entering into any particulars.

The letter, in a few days after, was given by Mr. Edwards to Mrs. Smith, the sister of Ann Saunders, and it was also shewn to a number of persons, most of whom identified it as the genuine hand-writing of the Reverend James Altham

It is worth observing, that when Mr. Lushington came to Ann Saunders's friends, to agree with them to have it given up, he at first offered her but ten pouds; however, her brother had the address to increase this price to sixty, which was paid in the course of a few days----and when finally given up, it was remembered, among other warm expressions, that Mr. Altham would never cease to love her as long as he lived: and only requested, that she would let him be an hour, or a night alone with her; he also asked her shortly after, whether, if he parted with his wife, she would come and live with him.

Mr. Edwards also deposed, that in conversation with the Rev. James Altham, he had confessed to him, that he was of a very warm constitution, and that he had been concerned with fifty women in the town and parish of Harlow; and as a particular instance of the vigour of his constitution, he further informed him, that directly after lying with Ann Saunders in the shrubbery, he went home and immediately obliged his wife to undergo the same proof of his amorous affections.

It is to be observed, that in course of this trial, several of the witnesses were asked, if they really believed that Mr. Altham was insane, to this, the general answer was Dr. Monro's excepted, that they had heard that he had been put in a private mad-houfe under the care of Doctor Monro, but that this was fufpected to have been done by his relations, merely to evade the force of the law.

William Poole of Sheering, farmer, aged fixty-fix, depofed, that he had been rather intimately acquainted with Mr. Altham, and that at the Tythe-feaft, at Harlow, Mr. Altham, after dinner; and fitting down with fome of the parishioners and inhabitants, introduced a converfation about dogs, and particularly faid, "that he had a great paffion for thefe animals, and women too;" to which W. Poole replied, Yes, Sir, I believe it, and you have paid for it lately, alluding to his connection with Ann Saunders. Mr. Altham then expreffed great virulence againft the people who concerned themfelves in that bufinefs; and faid, he would fhoot two or three of them if it was not for the law. To this Poole anfwered, he fhould not talk of fhooting people, though to be fure he was a man of great fpirit. That I am, rejoined Altham; and he immediately went on to tell them that he kept a girl when at college and even mentioned how he fupported her. He infomed the company at the fame time that the wife of John Wenham, Efq. was over head and ears in love with him; that fhe was at his houfe the other day, and kiffed him, and fmacked him, and called him her dear Jemmy, O my dear Jemmy! and the like; and that at Dr. Legas's, fhe afked him to have her.—To this one Edward Wife, who was prefent, faid in a ferious manner—Aye! what can fhe want to have you for? What, faid Mr. Altham, why to r...r her, to be fure. Mr. Poole then faid to him, do you confider that you are a clergyman, and a juftice of peace; I think this converfation may give you a great deal of trouble; to which Mr. Altham replied, he did not care for any body.

In the courfe of this evidence it alfo appeared, that Mr. Altham had been married to two wives, before the one he then had; but that he had treated them both with much tendernefs and affection.

Ann Tavner, wife of Francis Tavner of Harlow,

swore, that about November 1776 her husband was
arrested for debt, and confined in Chelmsford Goal;
and that when Mr. Altham heard of it, he came to
her to enquire into her husband's affairs, and said
he would do his utmost to assist him, or to that effect; and that he always promised to be a friend
to her, and particularly mentioned, that he would
get her husband out of goal in a fortnight's time.
After this, he began to call upon her very frequently, sometimes every day, and generally three or
four days in the week; still he did not procure her
husband's enlargement till four or five months after
he had proposed it. During this time, he had made
particularly free with her, taking very great liberties; such as putting his hands in her bosom, and
attempting to put them up her petticoats. In
addition to this, he very frequently solicited her
to be criminally acquainted with him, trying his
utmost to prevail upon her: sometimes, after
he had exhausted himself in persuasions, he would
even attempt open force; particularly one morning
in Feb. 1777, when he began putting his hand into
her bosom, and then tried to put it up her petticoats,
after he had unbuttoned and opened his breeches;
when she really believed, that if she had not resisted
to the utmost degree, by struggling and falling upon her knees with her cloaths under her, he certainly would have had the carnal knowledge of her
body. To this she added, that she thought his behaviour so barbarous, that she could not help crying.

Here it appears, in favour of Mr. Altham, that he was
by no means devoid of humanity, as he was so much affected by this behaviour, that he promised he would never be guilty of the like again, and though under no ac-
tual obligation, promised, and really effected, her husband's liberty in the course of three weeks. however he
had not quite relinquished his desire for the wife, nor for-
got his defeat some months after the release of her hus-

band, as he sent for her to inform her, he would send him for a soldier, for not keeping up his payments to him. But, though he thus disgraced his former liberality, he never put those threats in execution.

Thomas Speed, a malster, of Harlow, said, that walking one day in Harlow church-yard with Mr Altham, by his desire, he began asking him whether he had heard any thing of Ann Saunders's affair. Altham then told him, that he certainly had lain with her, and that she was very willing he should Well, said the other, and I heard that you found her a maid: 'No, by G——d,' replied Altham, she was 'as open as that pond,' pointing to a pond just by. And upon Speed's mentioning, that he thought this conduct very unbecoming in a man of his cloth, he said, in answer to it, that he was a man of a very vigorous and warm constitution, and that he had lain with a woman five times within an hour and a half ---He then went on and told him, that a certain lady not an hundred miles off, had been familiar with him; and that if discovered, it would cause a separation between her and her husband. This lady, the witness thought to be Mrs. Wenham. Mr. Altham told Speed, that he had not that experience in women that he had; as there was hardly three in the parish but would whore, if they were closely followed.

Mary Special deposed, that as Mr. Wenham and his wife, a Miss Nicholson and herself, were going to Hatfield fair, Mr. Wenham had dropped their company to speak to Mr. Altham, whom he saw in Hatfield church-yard; and that as soon as Mrs. Wenham heard his voice, she immediately went up to them, and in the hearing of all the company, said to the Rev. James Altham, "Sir, will you say that I kissed you, and called you my dear Jemmy?" and that he then made answer that he would say it: on which Mrs. Wenham gave him several blows upon the face with all her might; to which he made no manner of resistance, but only exclaimed, See! see how I am used.—However he persisted he would fay it again, and even take 'his facrament upon it. Mr. Altham's proteftations, notwithstanding, were totally void of foundation: and only add another melancholy inftance of the force of malignant difappointment, and exceffes, the fatal effects of thofe fituations, which people bring themfelves into, by giving up the reins of reafon to luft and fenfuality.

Mary Church, wife of John Church, farmer, of Matching, fpoke the moft in favour of Mr. Altham's infanity; and faid, that a fong was handed about Harlow fair made againft him; that he had often complained to her about it, and was very often much agitated in confequence of this fong. This, it is worthy of obfervation, is a new argument, which proves, that there is hardly any depravity fo complete, as to be infenfible to ridicule, whatever may be the vehicle by which it is conveyed.

Among other inftances of eccentricity in Mr. Altham, Mrs. Church mentioned, that he once called at her gate, where he kept talking and rambling from one fubject to another, for two hours together: he then mentioned, that he had had a thought of making away with himfelf; but that he thanked God that he had prevented him. That he likewife cried very much; and faid, he had done a thing by which he had difhonoured Mrs. Altham and himfelf very much; but that he had prayed to God, and God had forgiven him: and then added, I know he has forgiven me; and how do you think that I know it? I have lately had a large fum of money left me: and do you think that would have happened if God had not forgiven me?

In treating of the fong, we neglected to fay that it had a picture at the head of it with three faces, and that its title was, "The wicked Vicar of Effex:" the author was fuppofed to be a Mr. Whitnell, a clerk to John Wenham, Efq. at his office in the city.

W. Cotterell, of Manfion houfe-ftreet, London,

depofed, that one Saturday afternoon, Mr. Altham
called at his houfe, on his coming to town to do duty at his church the next day ; but did not then ftay
two minutes, appearing, as he had done at other
times, in a violent hurry and buftle, faying he had
a great deal of bufinefs to do. That between nine
and ten at night, he returned very unexpectedly
laughing and rubbing his hands, and faid, he was
come to fup with him, being the only time he ever
fupped with him in his life ; and then added, laughing I know how you tradefmen live and would not put
you out of your way and have therefore brought
my fupper in my pocket ; at the fame time
fhewing two goofberry tarts he had in his pocket.
Mr. Cotterell was much furprifed at his difcourfe
and manner ; but neverthelefs, making an apology
for taking him up two pair of ftairs, his houfe being then repairing, he introduced him to his wife,
whom he had never feen before. That he then
began laughing again, and faying what he had
brought in his pocket for his fupper ; upon which
Mrs. Cotterell obferved, fhe was forry he had given
himfelf that trouble, for they had a goofberry-pye
in the houfe, which was accordingly brought upon
the table. Mr. Altham declared he was uncom-
monly glad of it, being remarkably fond of goofberry-pye, and fat down to partake of it ; but foon
after calling to their maid-fervant, who was waiting, faid to her in the moft ftrange way, Poll come,
hither, my dear ? Don't be afraid, child, I won't
bite you. Do you love goofbery-pye? He then took
the two tarts out of his pocket, and infifted upon
the maid taking them immediately into the kitchen,
and eating them for her fupper. That, in order
to humour him, the fervant was obliged to take the
tarts into the kitchen ; but returning to wait at table fooner then he imagined fhe could have eaten
them, he would not be fatisfied till fhe went back a-
gain, and ate the tarts. He then began to talk with

Mrs. Cotterell, about his having a maid or two in the country, and he liked to make them a prefent now and then, and he bought a net-hood for one of them, which he would fhew to Mrs. Cotterell; and accordingly took it out of his pocket, faying, the girls in that country wore thofe kind of things, and they were very becoming, and he thought it would be a very pretty prefent for his maid. Then holding it a little time in his hand, he told Mrs. Cotterell fhe fhould fee how he looked in it, and thereupon put it on his own head, and tied it under his chin; and in that manner jumped and fkiped about the room in it in the moft antic mannner, now and then looking into the glafs, and afking Mrs Cotterell how it became him, and whether fhe ever faw a parfon in a net-hood before; and other expreffions in the fame ftrange kind of way.

After running on in this manner for fome time, and having drank a glafs of wine, he jumped up, and faid he muft go to his inn, or he fhould be locked out, and accordingly between ten and eleven he went away, defiring Mr. Cotterell to come to his church the next day. They went as defired, but Mr. Altham was not, at moft, more than ten minutes in the pulpit, and the whole congregation appeared in the utmoft aftonifhment at the extreme fhortnefs of his difcourfe, and the abruptnefs of his conclufion.

After church, Mr. Cotterell and his wife went home, and were fcarcely got into the houfe, when Mr. Altham followed them there, and faid laughing, "Egad, I have given them a bobtail; now I'll go to Woodford, and get a dinner at Keepe's for nothing (meaning a gentleman of his acquaintance there) and a good feed for my horfe, and be at home in a chevy:" at the fame time jumping about, and acting with his arms as if riding expeditioufly, he went away apparently in a violent hurry.

Hugh Tarling a bricklayer, of Harlow, faid, that when he was building a wall at Harlow, Mr.

Altham, ufed to be with them frequently, running on, and talking in the moft free and familiar manner, as if they were his equals, and would hand bricks to them ; and one time would infift on laying a brick himfelf, and then bragged how well he did it, and how clever he was, and could even fift cinders, or turn his hand to any thing, and that nothing came amifs to him.   That fome time, in the middle of his employment with the bricklayer, he would fuddenly, and abruptly fet off, and run homewards as hard as he could drive, and after being gone perhaps twenty minutes or fo, run back again in the fame mannei, and quite out of breath. That one morning he came, about four o,clock, and knocked him up, faying, he muft and would fee him directly, and made a frefh noife at the door.   That he then had his night-cap on, and his fword-cane in his hand ; and upon Tailing's going down to him, he found his bufinefs was, to infift upon his taking a little fence down, which jutted a litle into the road, and run on a great deal about his being a magiftrate, and he would have it done ; and if he would not do it, he would be the ruin of him, and fo on.   That after, he told him to get his hat, and go with him, which he accordingly did ; and in their way, ftopt juft by a pond in the road, and began talking about the prefbyterians, and Mi. Wenham in particular ; and complained how they perfecuted him, and that they wanted to be the ruin of him, although he wanted to be at peace with them and every body, and a deal to that effect ; and at laft worked himfelf up to fuch an agony, as to talk of throwing himfelf into the pond to drown himfelf.

Mr. Altham, at other times in his flighty fits would talk of the diffenters, and of Mr. Wenham in particular, in terms of great anger and refentment, faying, he would fight him or any man with fword piftol or fift, and would often run on a great deal in a wild and unconnected way, about his fighting

and running ; as that he could fight or run with any
man in England · he would then jump and skip about
in a very antic manner, and run and put himself
into fighting attitudes, by way of displaying his
skill and cleverness in what he was talking about ;
he was then very apt to swear much, which he was
never guilty of before.   And when he used to talk
of the dissenters persecuting and tormenting him,
he would burst into tears . and used to harp much
upon Mr. Parkhurst, his father in law, and Mrs. Altham ; and what a good and excellent man Mr. Parkhurst was, and that their was not such a person in the
world ; and as for Mrs. Altham, there was not such
a woman in a thousand , and if it was not for them,
he did not know what would become of him.   And
this strange and unaccountable conduct, in talking
and behaviour, happened, as Tarling thought, all or
mostly in the summer and autumn of the year 1779.

   With respect to Mrs. Wenham he said, that
finding Mr. Altham at Mr. Legas's the apothecary,
he began talking a great deal about that lady, and
how she had met him the day before at Hatfield fair,
and had beat him most cursedly, and very near
knocked him down, and then damned him and said,
"What do you say now, you dog?" Upon which he
replied, "Madam, what I have said I still persist in."
Mrs. Wenham then spitting in her hand, and clench-
ing her fist, attacked him again, and repeated her
blows several times.   Upon Tarling asking him
what it was for, he replied nothing, but because he
had said she had put her arms round his neck, and
kissed him ; and he then added, "By God, Tarling,
she did in this very entry : and to tell you the truth,
I believe what she wanted me to do was to r...r her.
As to her, she was a woman, and therefore I scorn-
ed to strike her again, but by God, if it had been
that potgutted son of a bitch, Wenham, damn him,
I'd have broke every bone in his skin." That he
then began to put himself into fighting postures,

and to talk and run on about his fighting; and how much money he had given to learn to fight, and of the ftrength of his arm, and that he was a very devil at fighting, and was able to fight any man in England, and a great deal to that effect; after which changing the fubject, he run on a great deal about his prowefs among the women, and that if it was not on Mrs. Altham's account, who was one of the beft women in England, he could do any thing he pleafed among the women, and fwore, that if he pleafed, ' he could r...r fifty or a hundred of them in a night,' and more to that effect: by every part of his conduct and difcourfe on that occafion, Tarling was convinced he was then abfolutely infane, and incapable of confidering or reflecting on what he faid or did.

Jofeph Legas, of Harlow, faid, that as he was riding by Mr. Altham's houfe, in company with Wenham, Mr. Altham being in his garden, called out to Mr. Wenham for his Eafter offering: upon which Mr. Wenham ftopped and gave him five fhillings; that Mr. Altham appeared much offended, and afked Mr. Wenham what he meant by offering him fuch a fum, and whether it was not meant for the clerk and not for him, and that he never took lefs than a guinea of a gentleman; and, upon Mr. Wenham's faying, he intended it for him, he flew into a moft violent paffion, and, his rage getting the better of his reafon, railed at and abufed Mr. Wenham in particular, and the diffenters in general, very much, fwearing violently, and at length ftripping off his coat, and calling Mr. Wenham a fcoundrel and a coward, and other names of that fort, challenged him to come down and fight him, and by fuch violent behaviour, a number of people were gathered round them. Mr. Legas afterwards rode on with Mr Wenham, who was much offended at Mr. Altham; and called him a rafcal and a fcoundrel, and faid he would bring an action againft him, for stopping and affaulting him in the highway; adding, that the fellow was crazy, and behaved like a madman, and other expreffions of that fort.

He alfo boafted to Mr. Legas, what a great dancer he was; and at other times has told him, that if he had been bred to the navy, he was the only perfon in the world for the king to have fent out to fight Paul Jones, and if he had, he would have taken him at any rate. That on thofe occafions he would always jump and fkip about, and act the part he was talking of performing. That at thofe very early and unfeafonable hours in the morning, he fometimes infifted upon his going home with him to breakfaft, and would make his fervants get up and get breakfaft, and after breakfaft he would go to bed again.

One morning in particular, as he was jumping and fkipping about the chairs, and bragging of his activity, he happened to fee Hugh Tarling, the bricklayer at Harlow, coming towards his houfe; he threw up the fafh, and called him in, when he ran on a great deal about Mrs. Wenham, that fhe was very fond of him, and vexed that he would not lay with her; adding, that he was the only man that was fit for her, as that fat-gutted fellow Wenham, could not half do her bufinefs; and then turning to Tarling, and catching him by the coat, faid, Why, Tarling, it is nothing at all to me, I make nothing of it, I could lay with a hundred women in a night, I could, indeed, Tarling, and make nothing of it.

But with all this eccentricity, Mr. Altham had his fits of piety; he would often deplore Mr. Wenham's defection from the Church of England; would even cry, and fall upon his knees, faying, "if Wenham would but turn to his mother Church, I would die a martyr to my religion;" and had often begged and entreated the witnefs to go to Mr.

Wenham from him, and endeavour to prevail on him to return to the church, which, to humour and pacify him, the other told him he would do, but never with any intention of doing it.

The firſt time Mr. Altham ſaw Dr. Monro, he ſaid he would ſhew him a trick by way of diſplaying his activity, which perhaps he had never ſeen before; then placing his hat on the ground, and taking up one leg in one hand, and pulling the other hand over his head, in that maner he hopped ſeveral times round the hat, and then ſtooped and picked it up in his mouth, without altering the poſition of his hands, or letting go his leg.—Very conſiſtent indeed, with the dignity of the ſacred function!

And by the depoſition of Robert Maſter, it would ſeem, that Mr. Altham, with his other fervours, had ſome ſmall ſhare of poetical enthuſiaſm, for being once at dinner with the Rev. Robert Fowler, at Harlow, he broke out in a poetical rhapſody on his favourite dog Zelio, declaring, that theſe verſes were the only lines he ever wrote, and that they were the effect of inſpiration!

Such was the aggregate of the evidence adduced upon a trial, which, for a variety of ſituation, circumſtance and character, has never been exceeded.

It does not appear, that there was any other inſanity in this caſe, than the almoſt uncontrouled dominion of violent paſſions, over a mind warped, but by no means devoid of ſenſibility.—There was by far, too much method in theſe proceedings for ſheer madneſs; yet, if any perſon would heap a greater degree of criminality upon Mr. Altham, than upon another perſon, an account of his profeſſion as a clergyman, it would be very unjuſt, and unphiloſophical. Nature is ſuperior to every religious form or inſtitution in the world; and whatever may be taught to the contrary, there is ſcarcely any virtue or fanctity unaffifted by the temperament and conftitution of the body: thefe, it is certain, are the ftrongeft influencers of virtue and good order, as that unaffifted religion, and education are the weakeft: hence it is a lamentable truth, that, in Popifh countries efpecially, the crimes and enormities of fome of the clergy, have only been rendered the more violent by reftraint.

Trial of Major Hook, for Adultery with his own Niece, Mrs. Campbell, Wife of Captain Campbell, before Lord Kenyon and a Special Jury, at Weftminfter, February 26, 1793.

THE Counfel for Captain Campbell, were: Mr. Erfkine, Mr. Mingay, and Mr. Holroyd. For Major Hook, Mr. Bearcroft, Mr. Garrow, and Mr. Burrow.

Mr. Holroyd, who opened the pleadings—ftated that this was an action, in which the plaintiff complained, that the defendant made an affault on Herriot his wife, debauched, lay with, and carnally knew her and took her away, whereby he loft the comfort of her company, to the damage of the plaintiff of 50,000l.

To this charge the defendant pleading not guilty, iffue was thereupon joined.

Mr. Erſkine to the Jury.

Gentlemen,

I am counſel for the plaintiff, Mr. Campbell; and although I feel on this occaſion for the unfortunate ſituation of my client, which my duty in this place naturally ſuggeſts to my mind—yet, if I could have diſcharged from my mind the painful ſenſations I feel at this time, by this cauſe being poſtponed or entirely put an end to, I ſhould have derived particular ſatisfaction as far as it regards myſelf: for I do not know any ſituation more unpleaſant, than when it falls to the lot of an advocate to ſtate tranſactions which bring a reproach upon human nature itſelf. If I prove what is ſtated to me, it muſt ſtrike at all the confidences and conſolations of the human mind.

The defendant, who is charged with criminal converſation with the wife of the plaintiff, is the uncle of that unfortunate lady—not an uncle by marriage, but her mother's brother. That, I dare ſay is ſufficient to engage your indignant attention in this cauſe.

Gentlemen, as I underſtand the adultery, the inceſtuous adultery is to be denied, and inſiſted upon as the principal part of the defence; I have not the leaſt difficulty in ſtating to my learned friend, that it will be abundantly eſtabliſhed in proof but although I ſhall make out to your perfect ſatisfaction, that in point of fact the adultery has been committed, I ſhall not waſte your time in making any obſervations on the nature of ſuch a caſe. All that I ſhall do at preſent, is to ſtate thoſe circumſtances which may be neceſſary to be known, in order to enable you to underſtand it.

As to the plaintiff, he is a captain of the 74th regiment, and was married to his preſent wife in 1786. She was bred up in the Roman Catholic religion, and was the daughter of a Colonel Frazer, who was in the ſervice of the Eaſt-India Company   This lady was religiouſly educated, and brought up in the ſtricteſt morals, although ſhe has not been proof againſt the ſeduction of the defendant.   In the year 1788, the plaintiff ſettled his affairs in this country, and was preparing to go to India, and it was then underſtood that Mrs Campbell intended to accompany him.   At the time that Captain Campbell was preparing to embark for India, the defendant, who is a Major in the Eaſt-India ſervice, came back to this country with a conſiderable fortune, and found his own niece (Mrs Campbell) under the protection of her mother, Mrs Frazer. the preſent plaintiff being abſent One is ſorry to lay any charge to any individual, I am ſorry to be obliged profeſſionally to lay a charge to any gentleman, and much more ſo, when it is a charge on human nature, which we all wear and carry about us. Yet I am afraid the evidence in this cauſe obliges me to ſtate, from the moment the defendant returned into England, he had conceived the diabolical purpoſe of debauching her affections from her huſband, with a view to that criminal intercourſe.   So early did the plan of ſeduction on the part of the defendant commence. that the huſband found, before Major Hook had been three weeks in England, a difference in the ſtile of the letters which he received from his wife. – She then began to ſuggeſt obſtacles to her going to the Eaſt-Indies   There was ſomething fretful and peculiar in her correſpondence, and he found at laſt, without any thing that ſuggeſted to his mind any criminal intercourſe, (for how could he poſſibly entertain ſuch an idea) but he had occaſion to ſee that ſhe was conſiderably under the influence of the defendant.   And Major Hook was propoſing to take a journey to Scotland. to ſettle a difference which had taken place between him and the plaintiff—not on the idea, you may be ſure, of any criminal intercourſe between him and the daughter of his own ſiſter, but a difference had taken place, becauſe the defendant had preſumed to give his advice with regard to certain matters, and which was contrary to the inclination of Captain

Campbell, The defendant had the art to procure the father of Captain Campbell, to infift upon his fon's leaving Mrs. Campbell behind him, and the defendant was to be a fort of guardian to her in her hufband's abfence.

The plaintiff and his father were at variance, and the defendant kept the coals alive —The defendant went down to Scotland and caried this lady with him . pretending to the plaintiff's father that there were great quarrels between her and her hufband, and that it would be infinitely better that fhe fhould remain with her mother, than accompany Capt Campbell to the Eaft-Indies. All this time the defendant was carrying on a plan of criminal feduction, which ultimately gave rife to this action —The defendant gained his purpofe, becaufe, for fome time his niece remained under the care of her mother The hufband went to the Eaft-Indies ; and the uncle pretended to live with Mrs. Campbell as a parent, at the moment they were carrying on this adulterous commerce.

Gentlemen, it is a very material part of this cafe to ftate that before the defendant had been three weeks in England, he carried this lady to Scotland, under pretence of carrying her to the plaintiff's father to reconcile her and his fon I fhall prove the defendant in fuch a fituation with her, and although I do not believe that the adultery was then committed, in that they had that criminal intercourfe which muft be the foundation of this action, yet it will be fufficient to convince you he had caft his eye upon her at that time, and therefore to that, all that happened afterwards muft be refered This was about three or four weeks after the defendant returned to England, and when the plaintiff was in barracks. It was at that time Captain Campbell faw his wife's affections alienated from him. It was at that time he complained of the uncle giving her fine cloaths Though he only confidered this as proceeding from the kind difpofitions of an affectionate parent, it was productive of extremely bad confequences to him. So far was the defendant from imagining that inceftuous commerce, that my learned friends come here boldly to maintain their client is abfolutely innocent, not only of the commerce, but that his mind or immagination never fuggefted fuch an idea to him. That, therefore, is the nature of the defence, that this inceftuous commerce never fuggefted itfelf to the imagination of the defendant, and that he is perfectly innocent.

It was with difficulty, Gentlemen, Capt Campbell could be made believe it, when he heard it the firft time in the Eaft-Indies, and immediately came home in confequence of the report. I am extremely glad, gentlemen, the caufe has not gone off. I underftand I have now the witneffes in Court They will be called, and they are many in number, I fhall prove firft of all, that they were found in fituations at Ramfgate, three weeks after his arrival, fhameful and fcandalous to relate.

I fhall prove afterwards that they were feen almoft in the very act of adultery, and that repeatedly, and if that is not proof fufficient, where fhall we find it? I fhall prove it was his conftant habit to fleep with her every night in the fame bed, the whole of the night.

It is to be reprefented, I underftand, that my witneffes come here to mifreprefent thefe facts They are unconnected with one another, they lived in the houfe with Major Hook and Mrs Campbell at different times. They are perfons over whom my client has no manner of influence, and therefore, unlefs you believe them corrupted with money, to come here to perjure themfelves in the face of God and man, to fasten an imputation on a man whom they believe to be innocent. you cannot refufe to find that fact, which is the foundation of this action

I fhall make no farther obfervations on this cafe It is of the moft ferious nature; like every other cafe. it muft depend on the complexion that belongs to it when you have heard both fides

I fhall lay fuch a cafe before you as I have ftated, my learned friend will then be heard on the other fide, and happy fhall I be if his client is not guilty, for every man muft wifh fuch a cafe was not proved. The evidence is of the strongest kind of any sort I ever received to urge on your attention.

Mr Cleeve, who was examined by Mr. Mingay, proved, that he married the parties on February the 17th. 1786, he said she was a Miss Frazer, the daughter of Mr Colonel Frazer. Her father was in India. He also stated, that the plaintiff and the defendant are cousins? And that the lady, when married, was seventeen or eighteen

Mr Campbell, first cousin to the defendant, and brother to the plaintiff, being examined by Mr Holroyd, and cross-examined by Mr. Bearcroft, said, that he went to France with Mr. and Mrs. Campbell, in 1787, soon after their marriage, in company with his own wife, and Mrs Frazer, the mother of Mrs. Campbell He lived under the same roof with them about two months, and never observed any thing but the greatest harmony between the bride and bridegroom.

Mr Bearcroft was very particular in questioning this witness. as to the behaviour of the plaintiff towards his wife but nothing could be discovered that was not consistent with the duty of a tender and affectionate husband —nothing that could justify—or even apologize—for the depraved conduct of the lady. He proved, that a bundle of papers which were shewn him, was the handwriting of Mr Campbell. He knew the lady before she was married, and, as she was only, he said, 15 or 16, he had no doubt, from that and other circumstances, but it was a match of pure inclination.

Elizabeth Henderson was next examined by Mr. Holroyd this witness lived as cook with Mrs. Frazer, in 1788, in which year, in the month of July, the family went to Ramsgate In a short time afterwards, they were joined by Major Hook, Mr. Campbell being then either at Chatham or Portsmouth. Their stay at this place was about ten weeks.

Do you remember, said the counsel, seeing any thing particular between Major Hook and his neice, Mrs. Campbell, during the period? When I went into the parlour one day, with a bit of bread to the Major and Mrs. Campbell, faid the witnefs, I faw the Major one hand round her neck, and his legs upon her lap.—Did you obferve any thing with refpect to her hair? Her hair, replied Mrs. Elizabeth, was rolled round his left arm, and his right-hand was in the handkerchief that covered her neck.—This witnefs further faid, that when the Major firft arrived at Ramfgate, Mrs. Campbell was very much alarmed, and fainted away at his coming in.—This circumftance arofe, no doubt, from the fudden remorfe of a troubled confcience, which at the beft of times, certainly could never be at reft. If fhe felt fo much at the fight of her uncle, who was a *partner* in her guilt, how much in truth, ought fhe to have been afflicted at the fight of her hufband! who, according to all the evidence, treated her in the moft tender manner.

In September the family again came to town, Mrs. Frazer and Mrs. Campbell going to their houfe in Brook-ftreet, and Major Hook to his own.

Jofeph Rippington was next examined by Mr. Erfkine. He was hired by Major Hook as his valet, in May 1789, at which time the Major was at the Bath hotel, cohabiting with his niece. After living here about three weeks, they removed to Sackville ftreet, where they continued about two months. At this time, it is to be fuppofed, that the lady had made her uncle as happy as this kind of connexion could make him, and yet is this witnefs fent to fcour the ftreets of London, to procure obfcene prints, which the Major faid he wanted to fend to India but, as will be prefently feen, for quite a different purpofe.

Did you buy thefe prints, afked Mr. Erfkine? I bought fome. I have fome of them here in my pocket of the fame nature. Now, Sir, did you ever fee any of thefe prints in the Major's hand?—Yes, I did. I went into the room one day——But did they expect you, when you went in? No, Sir, they did not, anfwered the valet. You went into the room when he did not expect you with a meffage; what did you then fee? Why, Sir, he

F

had got one of the prints, I had purchafed for him, in his hand, and fhe was looking over his fhoulder at it. When I came in, fhe turned her head away, and walked to the window.

The examination of this witnefs clofed, by his defcribing fome particulars of a journey through South Wales undertaken by the Major and Mrs. Campbell, no other fervant being with them except this valet. The Major, faid he, would not take any lodging at any inn, unlefs there were rooms adjoining, and a middle door leading from the one room into the other.

Robert Green, examined by Mr. Mingay, lived with Major Hook, in the year 1790, when Captain Campbell was abroad. He refided then in Duke-ftreet, Manchefter-fquare. When I had been in Major Hook's fervice about fix weeks, faid he, though before that I had fufpicions from what I had feen, I thought there was fomething going on that was improper betwen the uncle and his niece. One day, after dinner, more from curiofity than any thing elfe, I went up into the drawing-room, and I perceived Major Hook and Mrs. Campbell fitting on the couch which ftood behind the door, in a very tender way, with one arm round Mrs Campbell's neck, and the other up her petticoats. I plainly perceived Mrs. Campbell's naked thigh.

How fickle and inconftant is fortune! As a further proof it, we here obferve Major Hook at the very *fummit* of fenfual felicity, and in the next paragraph behold him in as critical and mortifying a fituation as a gentleman could well be placed in disappointment, chagrin, remorfe, nay, almoft madnefs, conflicting in the bofom of a beautiful young lady, while with a fatal weapon in her hand, fhe was feeking for *revenge* on him ! It is not for us to fay the firft caufe of this undoing ; but it feems to be certain, from this outrageous conduct of Mrs. Campbell, that fhe would, if poffible, have retrieved her honour, by facrificing her uncle.

One day after this, continued the witnefs, Major Hook faid to Mrs. Campbell, I am going out, and fhall be in at dinner, (the dinner was a cod's head and fhoulder, and fauce), Major Hook did not come in, upon which Mrs. Campbell waited till fix o'clock; fhe feemed to be in a violent paffion, and ordered me to take the dinner down, and faid fhe would not have any din- ner.

When the Major came home I let him in; it was a- bout half paft ten at night. He went into the drawing- room, after which I went down into the kitchen. After I had been there about a quarter of an hour, I heard a violent fcream and cry of murder. With that I went into the drawing-room, and perceived Major Hook ftanding in one corner of the room, with a chair before him, and Mrs. Campbell was trying to ftrike him with a po- ker. With that he defired me to quit the room, which I did, and went down into the kitchen. After I had been there about ten minutes I heard a violent cry out again, and Mrs Campbell ran down ftairs. This was a- bout half-paft eleven at night. She ran into the ftreet; the Major followed her, and defired me to go after her, I overtook her fome way down the ftreet. Her hand- kerchief was all torn, and the Major's waiftcoat was alfo very much torn For God's fake, Mrs. Campbell, faid I, confider what you are about, confider what condition you are in. You will be fent to the watch-houfe. On this fhe returned. She went into the parlour, and fhut herfelf up there. Major Hook faid, Herriot, I infift upon your coming out. She did come out, and ran up ftairs. Her foot flipped, and fhe either fainted or pre- tended to faint away.

The Major ftood over her, and when fhe recovered, faid, Ye wh—e ! ye d——d wh—e, ye worft of wh—s ! To which fhe replied, I confefs I am a wh—e, but I am a wh—e only to you. You, who ought to have been my protector, guardian, and friend, have been the utter ruin and deftruction of myfelf and family as long as I live.—Oh! my hufband !

No feeling mind, whether that of male or female, can fcarcely refrain from *pitying* Mrs. Campbell at this aw-

ful period of her amour; and though it is, perhaps, impossible that she should ever more regain a tranquil state
of mind, she may yet receive some consolation in the
almost certain hope, that the example of her fatal in-
discretions will operate most powerfully on the minds of
every female yet untainted.   While *her* story lives, and
an uncle dares make the smallest criminal advance to
his niece, we trust, that she would spurn him from her
with marked and inflexible indignation; that she would
not from delicacy, spare the viper, but instantly hold
him up to the execration of every one within the circle of his acquaintance.   Cuckoldom, in its best point
of view, is a crime of no common magnitude, it is
a species of robbery that would disgrace a highwayman,
for he boldly ventures his life. the seducer, who ventures nothing but his *money*, will send your wife panting
with pollution into your arms, when you take her joy-
fully to your bosom; but, if she does not *despise*, she
must certainly *laugh* at your raptures.

Do you recollect, proceeded the counsel, at any time,
when you lived with Major Hook and Mrs. Campbell,
that you had the curiosity to go into their bed-chamber
to look at their bed ? I do, replied the witness   A woman of the name of Betty White, who lived at No 18,
and who made the beds, &c. used to come down stairs
to me, and make me go up and look at Mrs. Campbell's
bed.   She said there had been more than one in bed:
and I always saw the marks of two

This witness confirmed what had been said before, of
the mode of engaging rooms at the different inns on the
road, and, in addition thereto, said, that one day after
dinner, while at Swansea, he was with the children,
Major Hook's sons, when he perceived the Major and
Mrs. Campbell lying on the foot of the bed in her bed-
room.   Here the counsel very properly asked, what pos-
ture they were in ? As soon as the Major saw me, I put
him into a surprise; he started up, said the witness, and
the flap of his breeches was turned down.   His face
was as red as fire at the same time he was lying in this

manner.—Did you obferve any part of Mrs Campbell?
Yes, Sir, I could fee her thighs.

Mr. Garrow crofs-examined the witnefs; and again
adverted to the curiofity of Betty White, who had invited him to look at the bed after the Major and Mrs. Campbell had rifen   He acknowledged having feen *fomething* elfe in the bed, befides the impreffion of two perfons; but, from delicacy, he did not point it out to
Betty White, who was ftanding in another part of the
room.

If perfons of a *fuperior* rank in life muft commit
crimes, at which juftice and decency revolts, how much
is it to be regretted, that they are fo carelefs of its publicity ! Inferiors will, of courfe, follow the pernicious example ; and having their mafter or miftrefs to copy
from, proceed ftep by ftep, till they imagine that to be
meritorious, which is, in fact, difgraceful to human nature

The wife of this laft witnefs, alfo lived with Mrs.
Campbell about fix weeks, fhe attended her to Swan-
fea; and gave fatisfactory information about the fituation of the fleeping rooms   Major Hook had his three
children with him, the eldeft of whom was eleven or
twelve, the two others about two years of age, thefe
children flept in a room between thofe of the Major and
Mrs Campbell and fometimes the eldeft flept with his
father.   The door of her miftrefs room, and the door
of the children's room, were left open by her orders. The
Major has frequently come in before fhe left the room.
Very often Major Hook, half undreffed, has come into Mrs. Campbell's room when fhe was quite undreffed.
but always withdrew when he faw the witnefs

Elizabeth Hurn, Elizabath Taylor, James Wood-
row, and William Lewis, all faid, that the Major and
Mrs. Campbell had been feen by them in loving, though
not in criminal fituations . they defcribed fome of the
Major's nocturnal *marches* from his own chamber to that
of his niece's.

Jean Grynds, examined by Mr. Erfkine, had lived
in the fervice of the defendant in 1792, as cook, at

which time Mrs Campbell lived with the Major   During that five months, tell us, said the counfel, if you faw any thing particular, and what? I faw, anfwered the witnefs, Major Hook and Mrs. Campbell together in his room, I went into Mrs Campbell's room. but fhe was not there, and in coming by the Major's door, I found it was fhut · the Majors room was almoft clofe to her's.   I had the curiofity to look through the key-hole; when I faw the Major lying along the foot of the bed ftark-naked as he could be, and Mrs Campbell fitting befide him on the bed, with her hand on his back. She, indeed, was dreffed, but the Major had no fhirt on at all.   While I ftood there, Mrs Campbell drew the curtains at the foot of the bed.   When I could fee no more, I inftantly went down ftairs.   The Major, previous to this, had been bathing.

It was admitted, in the courfe of the evidence, that Captain Campbell went into barracks in 1788, failed January 26, 1789, for India: and returned in 1792.

Mr. Bearcroft's addrefs to the Jury on the part of Major Hook.

Pleafe your Lordfhip

Gentlemen of the Jury,—The evidence which has been given on the part of the plaintiff in this caufe, entitles me to your full and moft patient hearing   My title I put upon this circumftance, that the cafe as it now ftands, is of a nature and of a complexion that muft ftrike every mind, as undoubtedly a very aggravated cafe And it is of confequence, that every generous mind will allow this follows when fuch a cafe is proved, that thofe who are to decide upon it, fhall well view and confider it in order, that the judgment, which they ultimately give may be temperate and moderate, for, unlefs it be temperate and moderate, it can never be juft.

Gentlemen, I fhould not be entitled to a moment's attention from you, if I attempted to diffemble the weight which I feel on my fhoulders.

The cafe which has been proved on the part of the plaintiff, has been ftated, and juftly ftated on this evidence in two very strong words—a cafe of Inceftuous Adultery. I admit it. I allow that fuch a cafe calls ferioufly on the feelings of thofe who hear it, and of thofe who are to determine, but it is my duty to remark to you, and it will be the principal part with which I fhall trouble you, to diftinguifh the fituation in which you ftand. You are not put there, nor does my Lord fit there, I am fure he will tell you, to punifh the defendant criminally, for any crime or any offence. Perhaps it might be thought an opprobrium to the common law of England, that it afferts no criminal jurifdiction of fuch offences But you will recollect there are particular jurifdictions, and different difpofitions of the power of punifhment, and different courts of different jurifdictions. Becaufe the common law has no fuch jurifdiction, let no perfon run away with the notion that fuch offences cannot be punifhed in England. Punifhed they are, and ferioufly. But that jurifdiction is in the ecclefiaftical courts, and not in the courts of common law. I wifh to remark to you, that there is another place where the criminal part of fuch kind of conduct is to be confidered

Gentlemen, my Lord will tell you, that the queftion in this caufe (I do not mean to trouble you with witneffes) for you to decide fimply, relates to damages what fatisfaction you will give by your verdict to the plaintiff.

Gentlemen, when I am endeavouring to guard againft mixing and running together different jurifdictions, when I am attempting to fhew you that you ought not to blend the criminal jurifdiction with the civil damages, you are to give to the party, I defire to be underftood, as not to be contending by my defence, that you are to divelt yourfelves of the other parts of the cafe. Take it as a matter of aggravation, but permit me to fay, and I fay it fubject to the correction of the noble and learned Judge, that you ought not, that you have no power, in the fituation in which you ftand, to give vindictive damages. Vengeance, punifhment for crimes, belong to another jurifdiction   You will take care in the verdict you fhall pronounce, that you wi'l not by any means mix other jurifdictions, which you have no right to take any notice of, with the queftion of damages which you are to give the party.

Gentlemen, it was ftated to you in the outfet, that it was underftood that the counfel for the defendant, intended to infift upon the innocence of the defendant, and to impute to the plaintiff an attack of this kind by the means of perjury.

Gentlemen, no powers, no perfuafion, after the evidence that has been given to-day, fhould prevail on me to ftand up as counfel for a party to attempt to do any thing of the kind.   It never entered into the mind of the defendant to give any fuch inftructions.   It would have been grofsly abfurd fo to have done   It would have been an additional offence, I confefs, on which to have founded an argument ; for, I fhould then have thought it an additional offence, to endeavour to acquit the defendant by charging the plaintiff with a foul confpiracy, with the intent to bring fuch a cafe as this againft the defendant, and fupport it by a variety of fuborned witneffes.   I difclaim any fuch idea.   My client difclaims it.

Gentlemen of the Jury,—having faid this, having marked this line, which feparates trial, judgment, and punifhment, from a queftion or civil damages, I am under the neceffity of chiefly relying upon that ground.

Gentlemen, with refpect to the damages, I have but few and very few obfervations to make.   The plaintiff quitted his wife ; the plaintiff went to the Eaft-Indies, and left her here.   It has been attempted to call a witnefs to prove, that he intended to carry her with him   As that is an ingredient for your confideration, I call upon you as a piece of juftice, which I am fure you will not deny me, to take that as a fact which is not proved.   I prefs my obfervation farther.   I fay, I have a right I think to afk you, and you will not refufe it, to confider it as a clear fact, that Mr. Campbell did not mean to take his wife with him, but to leave her here.

Gentlemen, with refpeft to the manner in which the parties have lived together, I cannot help obferving, that there is not that full and fatisfactory proof that might be expected in a cafe of this kind. Perfons who are near relations to the plaintiff, and others, feem to leave that liable to obfervation, and liable to fome degree of fufpicion. But do not underftand me to prefs it farther than is proper. I admit there is fome evidence of their living well together. And, perhaps, my Lord will tell you, when fome evidence is given, and that evidence is not contradicted, it muft be taken that fuch perfons lived well together. You muft take it fo.

Gentlemen, with refpeft to the damages you are to give to the plaintiff, there is another circumftance, which Juries, during my experience in the profeffion, have always attended to, and it is effential that they fhould; I mean the Situation and Abilities of the party who is to make fatisfaction. My learned friend, who never forgets even in the outfet to ferve his client's cafe, though fometimes he referves his ftrongeft powers for a reply, told you, the defendant in this cafe was a perfon who refided many years in India, and has returned to Europe with a great fortune: a defcription that was proper for Lord Clive, Sir Francis Sykes, and many other perfons, that we are in the habit of calling Nabobs That defcription however, very little fuits my client. Not a title of evidence has been given, not a queftion was afked about his circumftances, and my learned friend has fruifhed his cafe. Now as to that, he is a Major, and has returned home with a few thoufands in his pocket a great part of it is gone, and he is about to return to his former fituation in the army in the Eaft-Indies. It is in evidence to you that he has three children They can be guilty of nothing Thefe are the circumftances of this cafe. In affeffing damages againft the father, as fome of you probably are, I truft that is a circumftance which you can never be prevailed upon totally to forget.

Gentlemen, with thefe confiderations, therefore, I muft furrender his cafe to your temper and moderation.

I call no witnesses for the reason I have stated. You are in possession of the case. You will recollect, as I have said, you are not trying this man for crimes and offences, but you are assessing the damages that such a person as this shall pay to the plaintiff under all the circumstances that belong to this case.

Gentlemen, the doctrine which I take the liberty of impressing on your minds, is the doctrine of good sense, general justice, and I take the liberty of saying, that it is the peculiar doctrine of the law of England. I know perfectly well it is stated, by great authority, and we read in all books, that attention shall be paid in the question of damages, nay, even of criminal punishment and fine, to the abilities of the party. Nothing is proved on the part of the plaintiff but that this gentleman has resided some few years in India, and though a few return with great fortunes, others do not.

Gentlemen, these are the observations, that under such a case, I believe I have a right to make. I have been extremely diligent and careful not to make any improper ones. I hope and trust I have succeeded, because most undoubtedly, in a case of this sort, I am extremely anxious to defend my client.

I surrender him, therefore, without farther observation on the case, to your moderate and temperate justice..

Lord Kenyon's address to the Gentlemen of the Jury.

Gentlemen of the Jury—During the period of four or five years, it has been a painful part of my duty, too often to assist Juries, as far as I am capable of assisting them, in administering justice to the parties in causes of this kind. And if I could but promise myself that this were to be the last, that the reformation of the morals of the people might not be totally extinguished, to my mind it would administer great comfort indeed; for I confess I never did hear causes of this kind, serious causes of this kind, without feeling extremely for the distress of the party who has suffered this injury, and who has been obliged to appeal to the laws of his country for redress.

The manly, prudent, and discreet manner in which the learned gentlemen who has just sat down, has left the cafe of the defendant, has delivered me from the painful and odious task of drudging through that horrible ftory, which has juft been detailed by the witnefles who have been examined

It has been admitted that the cafe is proved, and therefore the plaintiff is entitled to your verdict, and the fole confideration is the quantum of the damages. You have been put in mind, and very properly, that this is a civil action, and that it is not a proceeding to punifh the party, as if he had been guilty of a breach of any criminal law of the country. But, gentlemen, when you are called upon to proportion your damages to the injury the plaintiff has received, I hardly know how to meafure out that fatisfaction in pounds, fhillings, and pence.

There are certain cafes where fome other mode of proceeding is to be adopted; but this action is brought by a perfon of infulted honour, and to whom no damages can be given adequate to the offence. The perfon who takes one's goods and chattles, is faid to have taken that which has been flaves to thoufands; but he that takes from another his good name, takes from him that which does not enrich him, but takes from the other that which makes him poor indeed.

Whether this action may not be refembled to fomething of the kind, it is for you to judge.

I fhall call back to you the outlines of the cafe, that which the plaintiff has enjoyed, and that which he has loft. you were told, this was a match formed in confequence of the moft ardent affection; that it was a love match, and as far as the fituation in which they lived together was difclofed, they lived in the greateft harmony and comfort till he went to India, and it was done away in the manner you have heard. But it is hinted rather than fuggefted, that fomething wrong appeared in the plaintiff's leaving his lady behind him.

What! has every young officer who is called upon to difcharge his duty to his country, the means of carrying his family with him? How few perfons are able to carry along with them all their comforts; and if he was torn away from thefe comforts and, if he was unfortunately torn away from thefe comforts here, is he to part with them for ever? Is there no hope he might be received into the arms of a wife whom he affectionately loved? Was he cautious and regardfull of her affection before he went abroad? Where could he have left her, except in the houfe of her own mother? Had he not a right to expect from the neareft and deareft calls of nature, that the uncle, the brother of her own mother, would have affifted in protecting her, that wanted the immediate protection of her hufband. But has fhe received that protection? I have a right to appeal to part of the evidence---fhe was a wh---e, a d---d wh---e, the worft of wh---es, fhe replied, fhe became a wh---e through his means that fhe was his only, and that he who ought to have been her father and her protector, had been the ruin of her and her family, alas! her poor hufband!

Gentlemen, did fhe fall an eafy prey into the arms of this Inceftuous Adulterer? As far as we are able to judge, all poffible means were firft ufed to corrupt her mind, in order that afterwards he might debauch her body Books to inflame her paffions, prints moft indecent to be exhibited by any body to any body, are exhibited by the uncle to his own neice, the wife of another man

Gentlemen, it is very true, in affeffing damages of this kind, one would wifh that they fhould bear fome proportion to the circumftances of the party who is to pay them. What his fituation is I do not know, but this I do know, that poverty, abject poverty, is no anfwer to a call of this kind, to a man injured to the extent this gentleman has been

I can point out to you no rule but that which has been fuggefted, certainly to confider it temperately, certainly to confider it moderately. But at what fum, temper and moderation, in a cafe of this kind, ought to ftop, it is for you to judge, and not for me to fuggeft to you.

The Jury withdrew about half an hour to confider of their verdict. and afterwards found for the plantiff damages,---Three Thoufand Pounds.

The Trial of Robert Newberry, for a Rape on the body of Jane Skinner, a Child about the age of Ten years. At the Affizes held at Kingfton, in Surry; March, 1759.

CHARLES Brooks   I am in the nature of a guardian over the infant Jane Skinner, who was then with her mother in Deadman's Place.   On Monday October 16, the prifoner came to me in London, to let me know the child was ill, and would not difcover what was the matter with her, till her papa came, (fhe meant me, whom fhe ufed to call fo)   When I came to her mother, I afked her fome queftions, but fhe told nothing. The grandfather of the child called me out, and faid fhe had got the running of the reins   The next morning I took her to Mr Hammond s, a furgeon and man-midwife, he would not examine the child without a woman; when the woman came, Mr. Hammond was gone out. Going back, I took the child into an apothecarey's fhop, told him fhe was bad, and defired him to let me have fomething   I faid to the child. Now, Jenny, I charge you to tell me what ails you, if nobody has meddeled with you, this will do you good. but if any boys have been rude with you, this will kill you   Then fhe faid, Bob Newberry had   The mother fainted away, and I was much confufed,   I called in the prifoner, and afked him what he had done to the child? Nothing, he faid; and I took him into a room, unbuttoned his breeches, and his fhirt appeared in an uncommon way   I fent for a furgeon, who is here and defired him to fearch them both. he did, and faid they were both foul   I took the prifoner before Juftice Clark   there he owned that he got this difeafe by one Peg Mackintofh, going to or

?

coming from Peckham Fair, or at the Fair, I cannot tell which. The child said, he put her head in a bag of wool, and put a *horn* up her belly, and wet her a little, that she cried out, Grand-daddy! Grand-daddy! Grand-daddy! and he stopt her mouth with wool.

Jane Skinner. I am a rug-maker: the prisoner was my apprentice at the time the fact was committed, I was next door at dinner, and had left the child in the care of the grandfather and prisoner. About three or four days after that, I heard the child complain that she could not make water. I sent her shift to a chymest, to desire to know what was the matter with her, he said she was foul, he gave me three doses of physic, which I gave her. The surgeon that searched her said she was foul. When the prisoner was taken up, he cried, and said he did it that day I dined at Mrs. Miller's. I said, When did you get this distemper? he said, as he was going to Peckham Fair, and that one Peg Mackintosh gave it him. I know no more of it.

Q to the child. How old are you?

The Mother to the Question. Ten years old, the 21st of January last.

Q to the Child. You are going to swear upon the Bible, do you know what is the consequence of taking an oath if you speak falsely?—I shall go to the naughty man.

Q What do you mean by the naughty man?—Going to the Devil.

Q Suppose you should speak the truth?—I shall go to God Almighty.

Q. Then you know it is a sin to swear falsely?—Yes. *She is sworn.*

Court. The conclusion of which oath is, "So help you God." You see God is to help you if you speak truth, but, if you do not speak the truth, God will not help you——Now tell us where is the man that did you the injury?—There he is, (pointing to him) his name is Robert Newberry.

Q. What did he do to you?—After dinner I was sitting by the fire-side, reading.

Q. Can you read?---Yes, a little.

Q. Can you say your Catechism?---Yes, a little. I was sitting by the fire-side reading, and Bob Newberry was at the window, says he, Jenny, there is a sway-butter without doors, I said, Come, will you go, he said. Yes, he would go and sway me. He went out into the shop to mend a looking-glass he had broke in the morning, and said he must go up for his rule. He said Don't come up after me. I was then about half way up stairs. He then ran down before me, and bolted the shop-door, then he shoved my head into a pack of wool and skewered it down, so that I could not see any thing. He then threw a great rug over me, and got upon me, and put something like a horn into my belly. With that I kicked him off from me: he pulled out a knife, and said he would kill me, and if ever I told my mammy, that knife should be my death; and that if my mammy went to Mrs. Barne's, he would kill me before she came home.

Q. That is in case you told?—Yes, my Lord.

Mr Donnelly. I am a surgeon. I was called on the 16th of October to Mrs. Skinner's to see this child; the three witnesses were all crying; Brooks and the mother said the child had been abused. The prisoner was there at that time. I examined the child, and found she had got what we call a clap. I asked her if any body had meddled with her. she said what she did just now. I then took the prisoner into another room, and found him very bad with the same disorder. I taxed him with putting the child's head in wool, and cover-ing her up after that manner. He said, he did not, but that he promised her a chaise, (or some such thing) and so she consented.

Q. How old is the prisoner?—*Donnelly.* Turned of 17.——He said he contracted the disorder com-ing from Peckham Fair, and mentioned the person that has been told your Lordship before. It was a clap; and it was just the regular distance from the time the boy gave it the child, to the time of its app aring.

Q. Could he give her this difease without lying with her ?—*Donnelly.* I apprehend he could not ; that would be a thing I never heard of.

PRISONER'S DEFENCE.

I never forced her in my life, nor never put her head in wool, or packed her up: I have been concerned with her four or five times ; the laft time fhe ftood upon two half hundred weights. She put me in mind o 'that, being concerned with one John Jordon before. Her mother has fpoke of it fifty times, or more, to people.

Jane Skinner, the Mother. I faid to the prifoner, How could you ferve me fo, when I never did you any injury in my life ? Did you ever repeat the thing before ? He faid, No, never before in my life. As to that he talks about Jack Jordan, my child was not two years old then ; and there was no more in it than that I am now in London.

Brooks. The prifoner cannot with fafety fay he had done it feveral times, as the child has been continually with me before fhe went then to her mother's. Guilty—DEATH !

Mr. William Bromel, a furgeon of New caftle, againft Sir M. W. Ridley, Member for that Town, for Criminal Converfation with the Plaintiff's Wife; tried in the King's Bench before Lord Kenyon, February 1793.

Mr. Erfkine and Mr. Shepherd, were Counfil for Plaintiff, Mr. Law for the Defendant.

Mr. Shepherd opened the Pleadings. It appeared from the declaration that this was an action for criminal converfation with the plaintiff's wife.

To this charge the defendant pleaded that he was Not Guilty, and thereupon iffue was joined.

Mr. Erfkine's Addrefs to the Jury.

Gentlemen,

I am counfel for the plaintiff, Mr. William Bromel, who is a furgeon and apothecary in Newcaftle upon Tyne. The defendant, Sir M. W Ridley, is a man of independent fortune in the neighbourhood of that town, and reprefenting it in Parliament.

Gentlemen, I am not inftructed, nor is it, I affure you, my inclination to go out of this cafe to make any obfervations, much lefs to declaim on the defendant, on account of the unpleafant nature of the bufinefs that brings us into a court of juftice. On the contrary, if I purfued my own inclinations, and my own inclinations are left perfectly free, I muft fay, that the defendant, in all other refpects, is undoubtedly a man of character and honour; and

he is married to a lady (I do not speak from instruc-
tion, but from my own personal knowledge of her
for a great many years) of the most amiable and
pleasant disposition. This is therefore, undoubtedly, an unfortunate cause for Sir Matthew White
Ridley, even as it affects him in this respect. I
have nothing to do with his sufferings, but ought
rather to turn my attention to the sufferings which
must be felt much more on this occasion by my client

Mr. Bromel had been married to this lady eight
or ten years and had a child by her, a daughter.
I am forry to remark, that my experience on this
subject is but too large, which arises from the depravity of the times in which we live.

I shall pursue this course. I shall simply state
what I am afraid my witnesses will prove, and shall
not give any gloss or colour to the subject, nothing
beyond that which I think properly belongs to it.

The wife of the plaintiff is a most beautiful woman, and when she was married to her husband,
was extremely young: and whether from any levity in her behaviour which makes a woman an object of temptation and suspicion, a report for some
time prevailed to her prejudice at Newcastle. As
I understand respectable witnesses will state this is
the fact, I therefore think it infinately better I
should state it in the opening, lest it might throw
any prejudice on the cause, which, when it comes
to be examined, will entitle me to call on the defendant for large damages in this case,

It is extremely true, this unfortunate lady, from
her own beauty and levity of behaviour, knew
she had subjected herself to such a report in a narrow circle, in consequence of some malignity which
beautiful women are but too frequently the subjects of. Undoubtedly such a report prevailed,
and within the knowledge of my client. I need
hardly state to you how much a husband must feel
on such an occasion.

"If I am broke in upon in the evidence which I shall produce in support of the plaintiff's case, I deliver up my client to be treated with all the contempt with which any man ought to be treated, if he was not watchful and properly jealous of the honour of his wife; if he was inattentive to her, and winking at her notorious adultery; or putting her into the hands of another for such purposes.

This report blew over, for a season she had lost the affections of her husband. A few more years had passed over their heads, and the plaintiff was living happily and comfortable with his wife, till his peace was broke in upon, and ruined for ever.

This cause was certainly not brought here for public example. I do not mean to insist upon it that this is any sort of persecution. I mean merely to state that this is the situation of an injured man —of an injured husband; and I think the injury sufficiently great, without bringing in aid any circumstances that might tend to inflame the minds of you the jury.

Sir Matthew White Ridley was not only a married gentleman, but was chief magistrate of Newcastle, at the time this injury was committed. He was also representative of it in Parliament. and, gentlemen, you will consider how much he has disgraced all these situations, by descending to commit a crime which is now the subject of indignation.

I understand this defendant comes here with this double sort of case. In these causes, what is to be contended on the other side is pretty generally known. We are first to have the fact of adultery resisted, and it is to be contended, that the defendant is wholly innocent of it If he is, we shall see it. On my part, I shall establish his guilt beyond the possibility of contradiction.

The other sort of defence is this. Adulterers do not frequently give themselves the trouble to enquire how far a woman is virtuous before the hour

of appetite commences, but afterwards ; and when
the husband is ruined, and his peace of mind de-
stroyed, then the adulterer is to hunt out what the
lady was. On this or that occasion she was supposed
to be this or that sort of woman in order to endeavour
to lessen the damages for the loss of her comfort and society.

I think this a wholesome species of defence. to wit,
if it can be shewn in a cou t of justice, that the husband,
instead of treating his wife with affection and regard , if,
instead of protecting her as he ought , if he is careless as
to her conduct ; if he permits her to misbehave : and if
he, as it were, encourages her in it, by conniving at
particular instances th t have come within his knowledge , if he delivers her over almost into the hands of
the adulterer, he cannot be driven out of a court of
justice with too much shame and too much contempt.
Though to Sir Matthew White Ridley, in former times,
this woman, from her conduct, had become an object of
suspicion , if she in consequence of the reports that were
circulated in prejudice of her virtue, had considered her
conduct, and had become more and more affecti nate
to her husband , if she was beginning, or had entirely
got the better of these suspicions; if she was the mother
of his child, and his affectionate wife in every part of
her conduct , if just as that sort of sensation began to
be felt by the husband , if just when he had recovered
his peace again ; if he was broke in upon, and made a
fit object for the hand of scorn to point out, (for such is
the unhappy condition of every man in the plaintiff s
situation however innocent) this defendant will have
much to answer for to my much injured client. If a
man happens to be married to a woman who misconducts
herself, and dishonours her husband's bed, let his conduct to her have been ever so properly and exemplary,
though he had afforded her every species of protection,
and shewn her every kind of indulgence that might be expected from a good and affectionate husband , yet the
moment she deviates from the paths of virtue, he instantly becomes the subject of scorn and contumely. I can-

not conceive a more cruel situation. I shall content myself with this fort of opening

The plaintiff was a moft affectionate hufband to his wife. He was careful to difcover whether fhe was faithful to him, and no proof appearing of her infidelity, he continued to cherifh her with that love, which his duty required he fhould. ·

Sir Matthew White Ridley, when he was mayor of Newcaftle, and had given the plaintiff a place under him, and had put him near to his perfon, took the advantage of that relation, to rob my unfortunate client of his peace of mind, and of that which was moft dear and valuable to him

I fhall make no farther obfervations on this cafe. The influence of the defendant, his life, his character, his fortune, are extremely well known to you, and from a long acquaintance with him, I believe him to be very much of a gentleman in all other refpects

I have confined my obfervations to the caufe before you, I fhall now call my witneffes, and prove my cafe

EVIDENCE FOR THE PLAINTIFF

The firft witnefs called on the part of the plaintiff was John Willon He depofed. that he was intimately acquainted with Mr Bromel and his lady ; that they always feemed to him to live in the utmoft harmony and friendfhip, and to have the greateft pleafure in each others fociety.

A few years ago, reports were circulated through Newcaftle, which reflected on Mrs Bromel's character and reputation. and which reports very fenfibly affected Mr Bromel, who fpared no pains to inveftigate the truth of them in confequence of the moft minute examination, and ftricteft fcrutiny into the foundation of them, he was led to conclude that they were perfectly and completely falfe.

Eleanor Swinney, was next examined in fupport of the plaintiff's cafe, and fhe was the only witnefs to fubftan-

tiate the fact upon which this action was grounded, name-
ly, the adultery.

She depofed, that fhe lived fervant with the plaintiff,
and that one night fhe found the defendant and Mrs.
Bromel together in the very act of adultery, on the ftair-
cafe in Mr Bromel's houfe, in Newcaftle She did not
difcover this to any body, till eight months after   The
reafon fhe affigned, why fhe had kept it fecret fo long,
was that Mrs Bromel told her that fhe would poifon herfelf
if the witnefs fhould reveal to her mafter that fhe had
feen her miftrefs and Sir M W. Ridley, in the act of a-
dultery.

Mr Law, as counfel for Sir M W Ridley, made a
moft excellent defence for his client It had, he faid,
been fairly admitted by his learned friend, in the outfet,
that the character and reputation of the plaintiff's wife,
had been extremely fufpicious long before the defendant
and fhe had become acquainted   And this was a moft
material circumftance for the confideration of a jury
It had alfo been very candidly admitted, that the Gentlemen of the Jury were not affembled for the purpofe
of trying the defendant for a crime , but the only queftion was (if they believed the fervant, who undoubtedly,
if credit was given to her teftimony, had proved the a-
dultery) what damage they would give   Even if the
Jury fhould be difpofed to believe her teftimony, he
fubmitted that this was only a cafe for very fmall damages

He remarked on the vaft number of actions of this
fort that were brought into courts of juftice, folely for
the purpofe of getting money, as it frequently turned out,
that the hufband had even encouraged and affifted his
wife in the commiffion of this offence   When that was
the cafe, it did not lie in his mouth to complain that he
had fuffered that to which he had freely affented , and
which, perhaps, could not poffibly have happened but by
his confent or connivance   He did not however contend,
that was the cafe of the prefent plaintiff

The defendant was a gentleman of high honour, and

had a large family of children by his moſt amiable lady.
The Gentlemen of the Jury were complete judges of
every cauſe of this kind, and he had no difficulty in committing to them the caſe of his client , being perfectly
aſſured that they would do ſubſtantial juſtice between
the parties

Lord Kenyon, in his excellent addreſs to the Gentlemen of the Jury, after lamenting the frequency of actions
of this nature, and the depravity of the age, obſerved, that
there were infinite degrees of ſhades in actions of this
ſort, and that each of them depended on circumſtances
peculiar to itſelf

In the preſent caſe, the adultery which was the foundation of the action, had been proved, if credit was given
to Mis Swinney It therefore ſeemed that the plaintiff was entitled to their verdict and the ſingle queſtion
was undoubtedly the queſtion of damages. He ſhould
not ſay a ſingle ſyllable on that point to the twelve Gentlemen who were aſſembled before him ‧ they were perfectly competent to the taſk of deciding between the
parties in this cauſe , and he could adminiſter no aſſiſt-
ance to them. It was extremely probable ſome of the
Gentlemen of the Jury were huſbands themſelves His
lordſhip deſired them to put themſelves in the ſituation
of the plaintiff, and whatever damages they ſhould think
themſelves entitled to in that caſe, to give the ſame to
the plaintiff

The Gentlemen of the Jury withdrew for twenty minutes, or half an hour, to conſider of their verdict, and
found for the plaintiff—Damages, Four Hundred
Pounds.

Trial of Mrs. Liege, for Adultery with
Mr. Wingtworth Tonge, during the
absence of her Husband.   In the Consistory Court of London, February 24,
1791.

THIS trial presents us with a feature of novelty upon
its very first face, viz. a Sailor's divorce, a thing as remarkable for its rarity, at least according to the forms of
law, as Sailor's weddings, without these forms, are for the
frequency of their occurrence.

Peter Liege, gentleman, of Broad-street, in the parish
of St. George in the East, aged 71 years and upwards
father of Peter William Liege, the principal party in this
cause, said. that in June 1783 his son was the comman-
der of the merchant ship the Kent, then bound to Philadelphia, and that when that ship sailed from England,
with many other passengers, there was a lady and her
daughter who went by the name of Taylor, but whose
real name he had since learned was Thomas.   Peter W.
Liege, he said, at the time of his sailing was a batchelor,
free from all contracts, &c. and that when he returned
to England, about a twelvemonth after, in June 1784,
he brought the daughter of Mrs. Thomas with him,
since Mrs. Liege, and whom he understood he was
married to about the month of September 1783, at
Philadelphia   At their return aforesaid, they took lodgings, in Broad-street, and lived and cohabited together at
bed and board, and consummated their marriage, having two children, a boy and a girl, since dead.

In the year 1787, it seems, that Peter W. Liege entered into the East India service, as mate of a ship, and
in consequence of that was mostly abroad, in parts beyond the sea, in his profession, till March 1789.   When

Mr. Liege sailed in the Nottingham Fast Indiaman, in March 1789, he left his wife in possession of his apartment and furniture in Broad-street, and Mr. Alderman Curtis, being his agent, had orders to supply his wife with such money as she stood in need of. Mr. Liege returned to England in June 1790, but as his father was apprised of the conduct of his wife, he no sooner heard that the ship Nottingham had arrived in the Downs, but he wrote a letter to his son, informing him that his wife had conducted herself improperly during his absence, and desiring he would not see her till he had first seen some of his friends. Of course he believed that the said Mr. Liege did not quit the ship Nottingham till she came into long Reach. He further said, that he verily believed that Elizabeth Liege did commit adultery with one Wingtworth Tonge, or some strange man or other, by whom she had a female child, of which he was informed she was delivered in Parker's Buildings, near Bermondsey Spa—And further, that his son never lived or cohabited with her since his return to England.

The Reverend Jacob Duché, of Sloane-street, Chelsea, and a minister among the people called Swedenborgians, confirmed the testimony of the marriage of the parties, saying, that being well acquainted with Dr. White, the Protestant Bishop of Pennsylvania, he very well knew the manner and character of his hand-writing, having frequently seen him write and subscribe his name —He therefore believed the Exhibit to contain a true copy of the entry of the marriage of the parties.

Ann Mitchell, of Lamb Green, in the parish of St. Mary Magdalen, Bermondsey, spinster, aged 16 and upwards, said, that she went to live as a servant-maid with Mrs. Liege, at No. 4, Parker's Buildings, who then resided with a man that she took to be Mr. Liege, as he always went by that name, and passed for Mrs. Liege's husband, but whom she since understood was a Mr. Wingtworth Tonge. All the time she lived with them, she said, they cohabited together as man and wife, and lay several times naked and alone in the same bed,

and, therefore, this young *del cate* witnefs verily believed they had oftentimes committed the *foul* crime of
adultery, and all that, &c.

Martha Moody, the washerwoman, next depofed,
that living in Parker's Building's, fhe was alfo engaged
to attend Mrs. Liege during her lying-in, and that when
firft engaged by Mrs Liege fhe underftood fhe was a
married woman, and that her hufband was to come to
her very foon. and that fhe was alfo prefent when Mrs
Liege was delivered of a female child, about four o'clock
one morning, in the month of September

She further mentioned, that fhe nurfed Mrs Liege
feven weeks in the whole, but, that during the laft three
weeks, a man came and refided with her, who called
himfelf Mr Liege, but whofe name fhe has fince un
derftood to be Tonge As in this interval fhe flept in
the houfe, and ufed to take the infant to its mother to
fuckle two or three times in a night, fhe had an opportunity of feeing them naked and in bed together, and,
therefore, fhe alfo verily believed that they had often
committed the foul crime of adultery together.

Henry Radford, furgeon and man midwife, of New-
ington-Place, faid, that on the 26th day of Auguft laft,
he received a note from Mr. Wingtworth Tonge, of
whom he had a flight knowledge, informing him that he
had a female friend that wanted his affiftance, and that
he was foon after introduced to a lady whofe name he
has fince learned is Liege, that fuch lady was then with
child, and very near her time ; and that he accordingly
delivered her of a female child. on Friday the 3d of
September following, about five in the morning in the
prefence of Martha Moody.

Mary Penney, wife of John Penney, taylor, of Bird-
ftreet, in the parifh of St. Georges, Middlefex, traced
the connection further back. She faid, fhe and her hufband lodged in the fame houfe in Broad-ftreet with Mrs.
Liege, when a perfon of the name of Tonge ufed to
come backwards and forwards to vifit Mrs Liege, and
ufed to continue, perhaps alone, with her a confiderable

time. All this witness then understood of Mrs. Liege was, that she was a married woman, and had a husband in the East Indies, and that she then appeared to be about six months gone with child.

Abraham Watson Rutherford, of Bond Court, St. Stephens, Walbroke, London, merchant, said, that he was well acquainted with Peter William Liege, on account of marrying his sister in 1785, and had known him in all for a period of 27 years. He perfectly remembered their taking lodgings in Broad-street, and cohabiting together as lawful man and wife, and their having two children—That Mr. Liege made three voyages as master or mate of different ships, leaving Mrs Liege in town during the same, and that on his departure the last time, he gave Mr. Rutherford 40 guineas partly for the payment of the rent of Mrs Liege's apartments at different payments, the remainder to be given to Mrs. Liege, at Mr Rutherford's direction. And he further understood from Mr. Alderman Curtis, who was Mr. Liege's owner, that he had orders to supply Mrs Liege with money to the amount of twenty or twenty-five pounds a year. And that whenever the said Mr Liege was going a voyage, he always laid in a stock of liquor, coals and other necessaries for her use, and in every other respect always made an ample provision for her, fully adequate to his circumstances and station.

During Mr. Liege's absence, he had frequently seen his wife in London, and other places adjacent, but being informed of her improper conduct, as soon as he heard of the arrival of her husband in the Downs, he wrote two letters to him, informing him of the same, and cautioning him not to admit his wife into the vessel should she come to visit him, till he had seen him, which happened on the 31st of May, when Mr. Liege came to Mr. Rutherford's house, who afterwards accompanied him along with a Mr Thomas Seddon to Mrs. Liege's apartments, when she, being taxed with an adulterous intercourse with a Mr. Wingtworth Tonge, acknowledged it before them all, and added,

in the prefence of Mr. Ward, a furgeon and man-midwife, that fhe was then with child, but at that time declined faying by whom.   This witnefs afterwards learned, that fhe was delivered of the fame about the month
of September, as aforefaid.

Such was the evidence produced on this trial, which,
for certain, has added a frefh inftance to female weak-
nefs when left by itfelf, and, in confequence of which,
many a fympathizing female in the fame fituation might
eafily adopt the following lines originally faid of their
great firft parent Eve—

> Lord! if the firft fair woman could not ftay
> In her bright Paradife but one poor day,
> How can it be expected we have power
> To hold out fiege one quarter of an hour!

A divorce was decreed in the ufual manner and form.

The Trial of Mrs. Henrietta Arabin, Wife of William John Arabin, Efq. of Moulfey, in the County of Surry; in the Bifhop's Court at Doctors Commons, for committing Adultery with Thomas Sutton, jun. Efq. alfo of Moulfey, in Surry.

THIS Trial, of merited celebrity, in the annals of
proftitution, for the audacious fcenes of impudent pro-
fligacy it contains, is the next we fhall offer.

Of the evidence produced before the Epifcopal Court,
James Bradley, a labouring man, of Moulfey, remem-
bered, that between fix and feven years previous to the
Trial, Major Arabin and his Wife came to live there:

he perfonally knew Thomas Sutton, jun Efq he well recollected, that one day in the fummer of 1782, as he and
William Harwood, a labouring man, were walking together up Moulfey Common, by a place called Littlehale's Shrubbery, William Harwood ftopped him and
faid, ' they fhould fee fome *game* '' and pointing into
the fhrubbery, he faw Mrs Arabin, the wife of Major
Arabin, on the ground herein, with her petticoats up,
and Thomas Sutton, Efq jun on her, in the very act of
Adultery, as he moft firmly believes, and when they
had finifhed, he faw Thomas Sutton, jun Efq get up,
and help the faid Mrs Arabin up from the ground, and
faw him button up his breeches, and wipe his breeches
knees with his handkerchief, and they then walked away
together.' he entertained no doubt as to the identity of
their perfons, knowing them perfectly, and it then being
a fine day, and he not farther from them than about a
dozen yards, he had alfo frequently feen them riding out
together, both before and after the ftriking circumftance
juft related

Maria Haynes, of Chertfey, perfonally knew Major
Arabin and his wife, and Thomas Sutton, jun Efq. a-
bout four or five years ago, being paffing through a
meadow near Moulfey Common, about two or three in
the afternoon, it being hay-making time, fhe perceived
Mrs Arabin and Mr. Sutton walking together alone, as
fhe had oftentimes feen them before, and prefently afterwards faw them retire into a hollow way leading to a place
called the Spa. Mrs Arabin feated herfelf upon the
bank formed by the hollow, and Mr. Sutton unbuttoned
his breeches, and gently throwing himfelf upon her, he
pulled up her clothes, and fhe plainly faw him in the act
of carnal copulation with her, being only about three or
four yards diftant from them, and concealed by the in-
tervention of fome trees and bufhes. Mr. Sutton, after
remaining four or five minutes upon her, got up, and
having raifed Mrs Arabin, gave her a kifs, and then they
went away together.

How fhocking muft thefe circumftances have appeared in the eyes of every friend and relative of this Lady; by whom she was really respected ! to have her conduct become the topic of discussion, in every gossiping circle, in every public print, nay, the subject of stupid jokes, and vulgar merriment among the lowest country boors ! how must vice have triumphed, when a Lady, formed under the extensive information of superior life, habituated to elegant delicacy, and checked by every circumstance of her rank and situation, could stoop to such vile indecence, to prostitution, unsheltered by aught but the open canopy of the Heavens !

James Poulter, of Vauxhall, about four or five years previous to this Trial, entered into the service of Major Arabin and his wife, as gardener and footman, at their house at East Moulsey an acquaintance, he knew subsisted between the families of Major Arabin and Thomas Sutton, Esq sen. who was Lord of the Manor, and particularly between Mrs. Arabin and Thomas Sutton, jun. Esq. Quickly after he had been in the family of Mr. Arabin, he noticed the distinguished attention which Mr. Sutton observed towards his Mistress, and with which she appeared particularly well pleased he oftentimes saw them go out in company with each other, during the absence of his master, arm in arm, in various places near Moulsey, and the scene of their excursions was more especially a shrubbery named Littlehale's Shrubbery, belonging to Thomas Sutton, Esq. His mistress used generally to ride out twice or three times a week on horseback, attended by him , and Mr. Sutton, jun used almost invariably to join her, and ride with her upon Moulsey Common , and if Mr Sutton did not arrive as early as Mrs. Arabin, she used to dispatch him home on some frivolous pretence, only that she might with more convenience wait for the arrival of her lover when they have been riding together, Mr. Sutton more than once kissed, and used other familiarities with Mrs. Arabin, on horseback ; such as putting his hand into her pockethole . when his mistress returned home, she has twice or three times told Mr. Arabin, that she had been at Siddon Wells, a place frequented by ladies for the purpose of bathing, when, in reality, she has only been in company with Mr Sutton.

James Lawrence Brown, came personally to know Mr. and Mrs. Arabin, by living in the service of George Molyneux, Esq the brother of Mrs. Arabin. One Sunday in the summer of 1779, or 1780, he being at the house of Mr. Arabin, at Moulsey, and his master and Mr. Arabin being gone out together, Betty Dodson, a servant in the family, told him, that her mistress and Mr. Sutton (whom he knew by sight) were in the parlour alone ; in about three quarters of an hour afterwards, he, being in the kitchen, heard the parlour door open, and going to see, just catched a glimpse of Mr. Sutton, going out at the front door of the house, and also perceived Mrs. Arabin coming out of the parlour . soon afterwards Betty Dodson called him into the parlour, and going in, he perceived one of the windows to be very much blinded, and an arm-chair near the window much tumbled and powdered, and several black pins upon it just before the chair upon the ground, he saw some seed or matter which comes from a man in the act of copulation ; on discovering the same, he called Betty Dodson, and pointed with his foot to the same, and she looked at it and smiled · from this he was in his conscience satisfied, that Mrs. Arabin and Mr. Sutton had had criminal conversation, and committed the crime of adultery with each other.

Elizabeth Dodson lived servant in the family of Mr. and Mrs. Arabin. Mrs. Arabin had one child during her marriage, and she verily believed that Mr. Arabin behaved to his wife in a manner becoming a good husband, and was ever particularly indulgent in his conduct towards her. Soon after she went to live with them, they went to reside at their country house at East Moulsey, and the frequency of Mr. Sutton's visits there soon became apparent . he and Mrs. Arabin found frequent opportunities of being alone together, and particularly when Mr. Arabin was out, which was generally the cafe in the forenoon, he being either on horfeback, or elfe obliged to attend his duty as a Major in the Horfe Guards : directly he was gone, it frequently happened that Mr. Sutton called, and foon afterwards he and Mrs. Arabin ufed to walk or ride together ; at other times when Mr. Arabin has gone out, Mr. Sutton has prefented himself in a field before the houfe, and Mrs. Arabin on feeing him, would wave her handkerchef to him, put on her things, &c. and immediately repair to him : at all times they were arm in arm together, and would frequently retire into a fummer-houfe at fome diftance from Mr. Arabins dwelling-houfe : oftentimes after their excurfions, Mrs Arabins drefs would look very loofe and difordered, efpecially her hair and head, though fhe was remarkably nice in adjufting her attire previous to her going out. One Sunday in the year 1779 or 1780, Mr Arabin and Mr. Molyneux went out together, and foon after Thomas Sutton, Efq came in, and went into the parlour to Mrs Arabin, after they had remained there fhut up alone for the fpace of half an hour, they went out. Betty Dodfon going into the parlour directly, impelled by curiofity to fee which way they went, found the curtains let down, though they were not fo before ; Mr Molyneux's fervant followed her into the room, and while fhe was drawing up one of the curtains, called her to him, and upon the ground clofe by an arm-chair, he fhewed her fome feed or matter, which comes from a man in the act of copulation, and afked her if fhe knew what it was ? And upon attentively looking at it, fhe replied fhe did and could well undertake to fpeak pofitively thereto, being a married woman the cover of the arm chair was very much tumbled and dirted with hair-powder, and feveral black pins were upon it, and from all thofe circumftances. Betty Dodfon was well convinced that Mrs Arabin and Mr Sutton had had the carnal knowledge of each other.

Towards the winter of the year 1779, Betty Dodfon faid, they ufed to walk alone in a fhrubbery very near to the houfe (the fhrubbery called Littlehales) and very frequently arm in arm ; after Mr. Sutton had gone, Mrs. Arabin ufed to come to Betty Dodfon under the fhed where fhe was milking, and fit down and compofe her hair and drefs, which at thefe times have appeared very much ruffled, though fhe was dreff'd very neatly when fhe went out. When the family was in town, at Major Arabin's houfe in Poland-ftreet, Oxford-road, Mr. Sutton ufed frequently to walk by the door and if the Major was not within, Mrs. Arabin would go out and call after him. Betty Dodfon twice faw them meet in the ftreet when fhe was going to market, and on their meeting they very cordially joined and walked off arm in arm together.

What excellent topics for fcandal, muft the proceedings of this frolickfome couple have furnifhed to the barren circle of a country vicinity, the retailers of fcandal, and the felf-appointed cenfors of morals, who abound fo plentifully in every neighbourhood, muft have obferved the ridings out, the fhrubby excurfions, &c. &c. and thofe decent little intimacies of friendfhip, the publicly faluting a Lady, or putting a hand into her pocket-hole to—look for her fnuff-box or handkerchief, with a fur-prifing combination of mirth and refentment the vari-ous clofettings of the parties of Mr. Arabin's houfe, muft have furnifhed a fund of the moft inexhauftible en-tertainment for the kitchen fire-fide, and contributed wonderfully towards improving the *morals* of the do-meftics of the family : how admirable an opportunity did the fervant of Mr. Molyneux difcover to difplay a joking drollery, when pointing with his foot towards the arm-chair in the parlour ;(from whence Mrs Arabin and Mr. Sutton had juft retired) he afked Betty Dodfon her opinion of a certain appearance very vifible on the floor! and how excellent an occafion did it furnifh to fhow her fkill and knowledge as a *married woman*, when attentive-ly confidering it, fhe found herfelf enabled to reply with fo much pointednefs to the intimation of the querift. Circumftances like thefe, muft produce in fervants the

K

profoundest reverence for the characters of their superiors, and wonderfully serve the cause of subordination: not to mention the happy effects the details of, and observations on, the principal particulars which come to their knowledge, may have with their intimates and perhaps on society, in a wider degree than may be at first imagined.

Thomas Girdler, a youth of seventeen, lived as footboy in the service of Mr and Mrs. Arabin, from him it appeared that when at East Moulsey, Mr. Arabin and Mr Sutton visited each other very often, and a very particular intimacy appeared to exist between Mrs. Arabin. and young Mr Sutton. Mr. Sutton, jun was very much in the company of Mrs. Arabin in the absence of her husband, and his attention seemed to give her a peculiar satisfaction. they oftentimes walked out arm in arm. and rode out together, and many liberties were taken by each party with the other on these occasions. in the absence of Mr. Arabin, they have been several times shut up by themselves in the parlour at Moulsey; after their departure, the chairs and carpet have been covered with powder, black pins. &c and almost always in such a situation, that some persons appeared to have lain on them whenever they went out together, the dress of Mrs. Arabin was particularly neat and smart: one evening when every person was out excepting this footboy, Thomas Girdler and his mistress, she sent him to fetch a pot of beer, and on his returning with it, she came into the kitchen, took the beer from him, and carried it into the parlour herself: about eleven at night he heard the parlour bell ring, and going in, his mistress told him to take the pot away, which he found quite empty; from which circumstance, and her not requiring his attendance as usual, he was satisfied that Mr. Sutton had been in company with her during the greater part of that evening.

On the next evening, Mr. Arabin being from home the boy suspecting that his mistress and Mr.

Sutton were alone together though he had not heard him come into the house, resolved to look through the key-hole; taking off his shoes, he stept softly to the parlour door; listening, he heard the creaking of a chair, and the sound of two persons voices, and looking through the key-hole, he perceived, by the fire light, his mistress and Mr. Sutton in an arm-chair close to each other; upon this, he run and asked a boy called William Charles, to come and see, which he did, and then they both looked through the key-hole; he was perfectly satisfied that the parties then committed adultery together. The next morning, one of the chairs appeared to be very much tumbled and powdered, with several black pins on it, the print of a mans foot on the whole sill of the window was remarkably plain, and that was apparantly occasioned by Mr. Sutton's getting in at the window, in order to enter the house with the greater secresy. Another day, when Mr Arabin was from home, Mrs. Arabin ordered the cloth to be laid for dinner in the library-room opposite the bed-chamber door: after dinner, she went into the kitchen, and told the footboy to get some large coals and leave them on the top of the stairs, saying, she would take them in herself, the boy saw no more of her that evening; the next morning entering the room, he perceived the carpet and chairs to be very much powdered, black pins laying about &c from which he was convinced, that his mistress and Mr. Sutton had been the whole afternoon shut up together.

During the family's residing at Mouliey, the footboy said, his mistress and Mr. Sutton used frequently to ride out together, the boy attended them, and was very often ordered to ride on and leave them alone: sometimes they would ride together till very late, and Mr. Sutton never used to accompany Mrs. Arabin to her own house, but always left her before they came near there; when she arrived home, she used frequently to tell Mr. Arabin that she had not met any perfon during her ride. When the family was in town, in the winter of 1783, Mr. Arabin going one day to Eaft Moulfey, he had not been out of the houfe long before Mr. Sutton called, and enquired if Mr. or Mrs. Arabin were at home; the footboy told him, that his miftrefs was gone out, and his mafter was in the country; but as he was fpeaking, Nanny Gatehoufe, Mrs, Arabin's maid, came running down ftairs, and informed Mr. Sutton that her miftrefs was at home, but that fhe was dreffing, and that if he would walk fomewhere and call in half an hour, he might fee her; he did go away, and returned in about that time, and was fhewn into the dining-room. prefently afterwards, Nanny Gatehoufe came to the footboy, and told him he muft deny Mrs. Arabin to every body but Mr. Sutton; he ftaid with her at that time longer than an hour, and, as the boy had every reafon to think, was alone with her during the whole of the time, in the back room into which the dining-room led; two of the chairs were very much powdered efpecially the back parts of them.

Thomas Parker, fervant to Major Arabin, was ordered by his mafter to go to the Parifh Church of St. Michan, in the city of Dublin, and examine the regifter-book of Marriages kept for that parifh: he found an entry of the marriage of William John Arabin, Efq. and Henrietta Molyneux, fpinfter, of which he took a copy, and then carefully compared it with the original: and he was well convinced, that William John Arabin his mafter, and Henrietta Arabin his wife, were the fame parties as thofe mentioned in the regifter. Thomas Parker remembered, when the family was at Moulfey, frequently feeing Mrs. Arabin and Mr. Sutton, jun walking arm in arm, in a fhrubbery, near the houfe, called the Manor houfe, or Littlehale's fhrubbery, belonging to Mr. Sutton's father, and at other places contiguous to Moulfey; at thefe times Mr. Arabin was generally from home. and when Mrs. Arabin has returned from thefe excurfions, her hair has appeared tumbled, and her drefs greatly difordered and rumpled, though fhe was very neat when she went out, which, indeed, always was the case when she intended meeting Mr Sutton.

One day, while the residence of the family was at Moulsey, in the year 1779, as Thomas Parker entered the house, Betsey Dodson, and Lawrence Browne, told him that there had been *fine work* in the parlour, between Mrs. Arabin and Mr. Sutton, and desired him to step into the parlour and see, on entering it, Thomas Parker perceived an arm-chair to be very much tumbled, and a great deal of hair powder upon it, just before the chair on the ground, he observed some wet, over which a person's foot had apparently been drawn, but what such wet was, he could by no means form an opinion by his own observation, as the same was nearly rubbed out on that day Major Arabin and Mr. Molyneux had gone out pretty soon in the morning, and did not return till nearly dark in the evening after the family's arrival in town in the winter of the year 1779, Mrs. Arabin used oftentimes to walk out attended by Thomas Parker, on the pretence of paying visits, but almost always Mr. Sutton jun met her in the street, and then it was their custom to walk together for a considerable time; on Mrs. Arabin's return, she has frequently told her husband, in the presence of Thomas Parker, that she had been paying visits to such and such persons, when she has, in reality, been the whole time in company with Mr. Sutton, afterwards she has dispatched Thomas Parker, with cards to such persons as she has told her husband she has been visiting with the view of preventing detection.

William Graham, gentleman, clerk in the office of Messrs Graham, Attornies at Law, Lincoln's Inn, proved Mr. Arabin's obtaining damages by action, in the sum of one hundred pounds, against Thomas Sutton, jun. Esq. in a cause tried in the Court of King's Bench, before William Earl of Mansfield, and a Jury duly impannelled and sworn : he also testified, that the copy of the verdict was a true copy. This was the whole of the evidence on the part of the prosecution, on the other

fide, nothing was advanced.　The Sentence was, that
'upon hearing the depofitions in this caufe, it was decreed and adjudged,　that Mrs. Henrietta Arabin be
divorced from bed, board, and mutual cohabitation
with William John Arabin, Efq. her hufband, and by
reafon of Adultery.'

To the particular obfervations which have occurred,
little more can be added,　than that on a view of the
whole of the glaring circumftances adduced in the courfe
of evidence, aftonifhment muft be the prevailing feeling
in every reflecting mind.

———————————

The Trial of the celebrated Mrs. Erring-ton, for Adultery with Arthur Mur-ray Smith, Efq. Captain Buckley, Captain Southby, Captain Roberts; the Rev. Mr. Walker, Mr. Trayte, Mr. Clarke, and Mr. Daniel.

THE firft depofition in this curious trial, is that of
Mary Stevenfon, who lived as a fervant with Mr. and
Mrs. Errington.　Her evidence amounts to this .　That
a Captain Smith lived at her mafter's houfe about three
months; that her mafter was in the profeffion of the
law, and generally left home about eight o'clock in the
morning, and did not return till four or five in the afternoon, or later; that during her mafter's abfence, fhe has
almoft daily feen Captain Smith toying with and kiffing
her miftrefs, and putting his hand in her bofom, and
through her pocket holes, at which fhe would feem pleafed and happy · at other times fhe has feen her miftrefs

fitting on the Captain's knee, with her arm round his neck
or on his shoulder

This must have created strange emotions in the bofom of the spectator, who was then about twenty-three
or twenty-four years of age. She doubtless imagined
something was intended besides picking the lady's pocket
when the Captain put his hand through her pocket holes.
Her feelings must afterwards have been greatly heightened; for, from the circumstances that followed, she
must have known that those degitations were a prelude
to a more capital scene.

She then says, that, " in the absence of her husband,
when Captain Smith and her mistress have been together
in the parlour, the little boy has been sent out of the
room, and she has frequently, after that, found the door
fastened on the inside ; and, her mistress hearing her,
would sometimes open the door to her, and sometimes
not, but give her some answer from within , and that,
when she has opened the door, she would appear rather
embarassed, her hair being greatly disordered, and her
handkerchief and cloaths much rumpled." She therefore says, that, " she believes, in her conscience, that the
said parties, at such times, were criminally connected with
each other "

After mentioning some trifling particulars, such as
those of Captain Smith going frequently into her mistress's
bed-chamber, and she into the Captain's, and that the
beds were afterwards found greatly tumbled ; she says,
' She has twice or thrice seen her mistress in the Captain's
breeches. coat and waistcoat , and that. at such times, the
Captain and she would help to undress each other.

Whether Polly Stevenson envied her mistress, we cannot undertake to say , but, it clearly appears, that this
toying between the Captain and her mistress, engaged
much of her attention, for she often watched them into
the hay-loft together, whither they repaired under pretence of finding eggs ; and she says, ' Her mistress, when
she returned, had her cloaths much tumbled, and in great
disorder.' At those times she says, ' She had no doubt

upon her mind, that the said parties had a criminal connection "

Mrs. Polly also watched the waters of the poor curate of Batterfea. Cruel, indeed, that he could not be admitted to give her miftrefs a little fpiritual confolation, but fhe muft put a carnal conftruction upon his intentions. She fays, ' She faw Mr. Walker and her miftrefs come out of the bed-chamber together,' and without further evidence of any thing criminal fhe runs immediately to the kitchen and tells her fellow fervants, that fhe believed ' the parfon and her miftrefs had been in a fit together on the bed.'

How depraved muft the mind of Polly Stevenfon have been, to form fuch a fuppofition ! Does fhe imagine that nothing but carnalities can be practifed in a bedroom ? Might not he and Mrs. Errington, who was one of his parifhoners, have been joining in fome religious exerciles, inftead of perpetrating the horrid crime of adultery ? Might they not have been conning over the ' leffons of the day,' and turning over the fheet of the ' Pilgrim's Progrefs ?' Might he not have pulled out of his pocket ' The Whole Duty of Man,' and have pointed out particular interefting practical paffages ! Was he not, thought in a fubordinate degree, the fhepherd of the parifh , and was not fhe one of his lambs ?—But, if a tranfaction will bear two conftructions, Polly feems to delight in giving it the worft. It is poffible that, having a ftrong tendency to fornication herfelf, fhe fuppofes a ' pair of people' cannot go into a ' bed-room' without committing adultery , and actually fays, that ' fhe firmly believes that a criminal connection had paffed between them.' She does not indeed mention the grofs and indelicate words, ' carnal knowledge.'

She then relates that ' her miftrefs, being once in a coach with her, put her head out of the window, and afked a fmart officer how he did, and he came up to the coach, and the coach ftopped, and he opened the door and got in , and Mrs. Errington carried him to her hufband's houfe, where he ftaid to tea, and continued alone

with her in the parlour some time ; and that, from their
converfation it appeared, that fuch officer was an entire
ftranger to Mrs. Errington. That a great intimacy afterwards took place between them, and it appeared that
this officer's name was Buckley.

The Captain made his attacks in nearly the fame order as Captain Smith, and in particular, regularly befieg-
ed the bofom and the pocket-holes Mary Stephenfon
obferves alfo, that, 'whilft her mafter was on a journey
to Oxford, her miftrefs ftaid out all night twice,' and
feems to conjecture that captain Buckley was with her.

Jacob Endamaur comes forward as the next witnefs,
and fays, ' he was a fervant to Mr and Mrs. Errington,
and has frequently feen Captain Smith and his miftrefs
kiffing, toying, and romping together, and has feen his
miftrefs fitting upon the Captain's knee, and her hair and
cloaths in great diforder.' He makes no criminal
charge againft the curate, but only fays, he ufed now
and then to vifit and drink tea at the houfe of his faid
mafter, and that he never faw any thing improper pafs
between him and his miftrefs '

He then confirms the evidence given by Mary Stevenfon, refpecting captain Buckley, and adds, that
' about two months before he left Mr. Errington's
fervice, as he went into the parlour, where Captain
Buckley and his miftrefs were alone together, to
throw fome coals on the fire, and entering rather
fuddenly, he faw his miftrefs fitting in an elbow-
chair, and Captain Buckley ftanding before her ;
that upon his coming in, Captain Buckly turned
immediately away, and appeared to be buttoning
up his breeches ; and they appeared to be in very
great confufion.'

Hence he concludes, that ' they either had been,
or were prevented by him from being, criminally
acquainted together.'

Thofe, however, who pretend to be in the fecret affirm, that nothing of that kind was then
tranfacting ; but the lady was adminiftering fome-

thing to the Captain, in a particular part, to deftroy a fpecies of teftaceous infects, which were at that time very troublefome and inconvenient to him. She was acting, it is prefumed, the part of ' Lady Bountiful,' by endeavouring to deftroy fuch noxious vermin , and yet Jacob Endamaur moft uncharitably conjectures, that fhe was engaged with the Captain in bufinefs of a very different nature !

He adds, that ' he has often feen them kiffing and fondling each other ; and once faw the Captain kiffing her naked breaft ' He concludes with faying, ' that he does in his confcience believe, that the faid parties had frequently had the carnal knowledge of each other.'

Philip Dixon, clerk to Mr. Errington, befides confirming fome of the particulars already mentioned, depofes, that captain Buckley, at firft, ' would ftand in a lane juft by the houfe, as if upon the watch and, upon thofe occafions, Mrs. Errington would go to him, and bring him home, or ftay fome time with him, and he has known her ftay in the lane with him till eleven o clock at night. That at length, the Captain grew more audacious in his behavior, and would come within about a quarter of an hour after Mr Errington was gone out ; and, without afking any queftions, would run up ftairs, whiftling or finging, into Mrs Errington's bed-chamber, dreffing-room, or parlour, wherever fhe happened to be. That once, in particular, he remembers Captain Buckley and Mrs. Errington coming into a room called the library, where the deponent ufually fat to write, and while they were in the room, the Captain went up to her in a very familiar manner, and, as fhe retired backwards, he followed her until fhe came with her back againft the bookcafe, and then pufhed his hand in a moft indecent manner, againft her cloaths, between her thighs, and Mrs. Errington gently pufhed him from her, and they both went out of the room.

Thefe particulars are fo very open and apparent, as to require very little comment or elucidation. Mrs. Errington, on their firft interview, behaves with great freedom to the Captain; and he in his turn seems to have exactly followed her example In short he acted as master of the house, and one would imagine he really thought himself so; but his audacity at last was insupportable, Mr Philip Dixon therefore. communicated his suspicions, or rather facts, to Mr Errington, and a seperation consequently took place between him and his wife, and Mr. Dixon believes that Mr. Errington has never since cohabited with her.

Another circumstance of her behaviour, mentioned by Mr Dixon. is too material to be ommitted He says, ' Mr Errington's house in Adam-street, was exactly faceing the hotel. kept by William Osborne, in the same street, and that Mrs Errington. when her husband was absent upon business, very frequently went out and staid for hours together, and often used to return home with various gentlemen strangers to the deponent. and appeared but newly acquainted with Mrs Errington

There never was a more industrious woman in her line. than our heroine Idleness she seems to have had an aversion to. and upon all occasions preferred an active life Her generosity too was unbounded, she did not confine herself to a small circle, and deal out favours with a parsimonious hand. but liberally distributed them to every one that asked, and frequently even unasked. If the riches of a kingdom depends upon its population. (a point in which all our politicians seem to be agreed, Mrs Errington must certainly be a valuable member of society, her whole time is employed in the business of procreation, and she constantly exerts her best endeavours to make new subjects for the state She has not, indeed. been very successful in her endeavours, therefore she may exclaim, in the language of Addison,

" 'Tis not in mortals to command success,
" But we'll do more, Sempronius, we'll deserve it '
CATO

It is however a just and a general observation, that

the ladies who labour too hard in the bufinefs of propa-gation, feldom propagate much. This appears to be precifely the cafe in the prefent inftance ; and, if every woman was as indefatigable in this bufinefs as Mrs. Er-rington, the king might 'lack foldiers, and failors,' which would be a heavy lofs at this moment.

Luke Carter comes forward next with his teftimony. He was alfo a fervant to Mr. and Mrs. Errington. He fays Captain Smith and his miftrefs ufed to romp, play, and toy together ; and goes upon the fame ground as the reft of the witneffes ; but fays nothing new, except that the Captain ufed to chuck his miftrefs under the chin, and gently fqueeze her hand. Luke appears to be an arch fellow, and feems to h ve a particular allufion when he mentions the Captain s ' playing at chuck un-der the chin.' Probably it was at fome confiderable dif-tance *under* the chin !

Simon Orchard, aged fixteen years, is the next wit-nefs. He was foot-boy to Mr. Branfton, in Lyme-Re-gis, at a time when Mrs Errington boarded there. He depofes that, ' being one day in his mafter's parlour upon fome errand, Mrs Errington called him to her, and taking a book out of her pocket, fhewed him feveral in-cent pictures therein, exhibiting the private parts of both fexes, which fhe particularly pointed out to him, and told him, fuch pictures were a reprefentation of the feveral methods in which gentle-folks and poor folks were connected together.

Mrs. Errington, it muft be acknowledged, had always an eye to bufinefs, and as poor fimple Simon was, at that time, only fixteen years of age, fhe was apprehenfive that he m ght have been daunted, had fhe proceeded in a more direct manner. She was determined, however, to have a relifh of him, and her mode of angling for him was truly ingenious.

Simon proceeds with his evidence, and fays that, ' a-bout two days afterwards, as one Mr. Daniel, an attor-ney's clerk in the town, was paffing by on horfeback, Mrs. Errington tapped againft the parlour window, and

Mr. Daniel immediately alighted, tied up his horfe at the door, and walked in, when Mrs. Errington met him at the door, and afked him to take a walk round the garden, and they accordingly walked together in the orchard behind the houfe, and Simon afterwards faw them fitting upon the grafs, but, on their obferving him, fhe came and beat him about the head for watching them, and then returned to Mr Daniel.'

He then relates, that a Captain Roberts, and a Captain Southby, had practifed great familiarities with Mrs. Errington, and from their having been fhut up in rooms together, he fuppofes they at thofe times committed adultery.

He next depofes, that ' Mr Trayte, poftmafter of Lyme, vifited Mrs. Errington, and they behaved with great familiarity to each other, that he faw them playing in the orchard together and when Mis Errington ran round the trees, Mr Trayte purfued her till fhe fell down, and he then caught hold of her, and fhe faid he had hurt her leg, and pulled her petticoats above her knee, and Mr. Trayte put his hand upon her knee: that he then affifted her in getting up, and fhe ran and fell again and pulled up her petticoats nearly as high as fhe had done before, that, about half an hour afterwards, they got into the kitchen together, and Mrs. Errington went into the ftore-room and fetched a fyringe, which Mr Trayte took from her and filled it with water, and difchaiged it under her petticoats "

This appears to have been a very extraordinary kind of amufement for Mr. Trayte. After having juft had two views above the lady's knee, it is impoff.ble to conceive why he fhould have recourfe to a pewter fquirt, and to difcharge the contents of it under her petticoats He may be a tolerable good ' Poftmafter,' but he muft be a wretched ' wh——e-mafter,' not to think of a better expedient to cool the lady's warm premifes. Had either of her Captain's been then upon duty, they would have acted more ' en militaire ' The poft mafter of Lyme-Regis ftands but a poor chance of obtaining a wife (if he has not already got one) for having worked an improper 'engine,' and treated a very 'reverend' looking figure with unbecoming levity.

Soon after this, a very cruel disaster happened to poor Simon and such a one as fully retaliated for his watching Mr. Trayte and Mrs. Errington   The poor fellow depoſes, that 'the next night as he was asleep in his bed, he was waked by the bedcloaths being striped off him, and observed Mrs. Errington in her shift only, and Phebe Lush, which then lived fellow servant with him, by his bed-side, and Mrs. Errington pulled up his shirt and caught hold of his private parts, and pulled him out of bed by the same, and said she would pull him down stairs, but he at length got away from her by tearing down the bosom of her shift.

Alas, poor Simon! If you had not been looked upon as a youth of veracity, I should hardly have credited such a tale; this being the first time, by what I can learn, that Mrs. Errington attempted to treat such, 'matters' with diſreſpect, much less with a degree of cruelty. But the most astonishing part of this transaction is, that, after having taken a 'thing in hand, she could ever think of quitting the room till she had finished it —Perhaps she is not fond of miniatures

'The next night, continues master Simon, 'just as he had undreſſed himself and was going into the bed, Mrs. Errington came into the room, and made him put on his breeches, and then took him down stairs into her bed-chamber, and placed him under the bedstead of his fellow-servant, Mary Mitchell, which stood even with Mrs. Errington's bed, and bade him hide himself till the said Mary Mitchell should come to bed, and was gone to sleep, and that she would then speak to him

But when the mistreſs and maid were undreſſing to go to bed, the maid heard something breathe hard, and, by the help of the candle, she discovered poor Simon, and sent him to his own bed '

Poor Simon muſt have thought himself in a very whimsical situation, when placed under Mary Mitchell's bedstead.   He was not so entirely an infant, as not to be able to form some imperfect idea of what Mrs Errington meant, when she said she would ' speak to him after Mary Mitchell was gone to sleep ' Simon could not, at that early period be ignorant of the mode of gestation, though perhaps he had then only a theoretical knowledge of it, and he must have been well convinced, that Mrs. Errington intended he should attempt the practical part It seems evident indeed, that Simon experienced those sensations which such a situation must naturally create, and that he was amply supplied with materials to act the part of a man, or he would not so readily and quietly have complied with the lady's injunctions of crawling under the bedstead, and to continue in that disagreeable hiding-place, till she ordered him to mount   In the words of the poet Mrs Errington wanted

" To teach the young idea how to shoot '

But it does not appear, from the evidence given that he was led out of the room in the same manner that he was taken out of bed by Mrs Errington

The next morning, as master Simon deposes, ' he saw Mrs Errington standing before the fire with her petticoats as high as her knees, in the presence of Phebe Tush, Mary Mitchell, and his master's son, who was then about five years of age, and, seeing some hair lying upon a paper, asked what it was, and the little boy said Mrs Errington had been cutting it off under her petticoats, and then asked Mrs Errington to give him some, when she replied, if she cut off any more, Mr. Errington would know it '

Thus closes the evidence of master Simon   but there appears a deficiency in his deposition, for he does not mention a syllable about the colour of this hair.

Mrs Errington appears upon all occasions, to consider the propriety of her actions   She did not choose to part with a hair more, lest it should be missed by her husband, but she never thought it necessary to refuse those favours that could not be missed by Mr. Errington, though of ten thousand times the value

Phebe Lush is the next witness on the trial; she corroborates what Simon Orchard had deposed, respecting the mode of Mrs. Errington's dragging him out of bed by the middle; she also mentions Mrs. Errington's shewing her some indecent pictures; and she adds that, 'one day in the kitchen, she, in a very indecent manner took up her petticoats, and, with a pair of scissars, cut off some hair from her private parts, and gave some to Mary Mitchell, and some to this deponent, and bade them keep for her sake; and, to the best of this deponent's rememberance, Simon Orchard, the foot-boy, came into the kitchen whilst she was about it.'

It seems perfectly clear, from what has been already advanced, that the first tuft of hair which was generously bestowed by Mrs Errington, to those about her, was all taken from one side of the premises, and the beard appearing afterwards to be rather unequally divided, she gave it a second 'mowing,' in order to bring matters into a due proportion and uniformity.

Mary Mitchell next steps forward with her testimony. She was cook to Mr. Branston when Mrs Errington boarded at his house. She corroborates the evidence given by several others, and adds, that Mr. Clarke, one afternoon amused himself with taking off Mrs Errington's stockings, and putting them on again, frequently kissing her.'

This was a strange kind of penchant of Mr. Clarke's! —'Pulling off her stockings and putting them on again! It reminds us of Motteux, who translated Don Quixote. He had a strong propensity to women but, as he advanced in years, he found it necessary to have recourse to art to give him ability as well as inclinations. We never heard, indeed, that he had recourse to the manœuvre of practising upon legs and stockings, like Mr. Clarke; but he had other methods equally extraordinary; and, at length, Nature became so far debilitated, that nothing but hanging by the neck for a few moments, would give him that elasticity necessary for consummation. Extraordinary as it may appear, he frequently submitted to this operation, in order to procure a gratification, which, like Mrs. Errington, he considered as the only business worth attending to. At length, however, his life became a forfeit for his imprudence.——He was tuck'd up as usual in a two pair of stairs room, in the presence of three ' filles des joye ;' and, just as he was suspended, hearing that some dancing bears were performing in the street, they all ran down to enjoy a sight of the entertainment, and, forgetting, for a while, the situation in which they had left Monsieur Motteux, when they returned, they immediately cut him down, but he was totally incapacitated for business, and also dead! Thus also, died the musician KOTSWARRA, whose exploits are so brilliantly recorded in a new publication called Modern Propensities.

Mary Mitchell mentions several particulars, which have already been fully related, and, further observes, that, when Mrs. Errington showed the obscene pictures, she would talk in a very immodest manner.

The same witness also says, that ' Captain Southby and Mrs. Errington being in a room together, she tried at the door, and found it fastened, or locked within side; that Mrs. Errington called from within, and asked her what she wanted, and Mary Mitchell told her the dinner was ready, and she told the deponent it must wait, for she was not ready for it yet, that, in the course of half an hour more, Mrs. Errington and Captain Southby came out of the parlour, and the latter went immediately away, that Mrs. Errington appeared quite heated, and looked confused, and her hair and cap, and the handkerchief about her neck were in great disorder, that she had no stays on, being in her morning dress, which appeared very much tumbled '——She adds that, ' she afterwards found the carpet much tumbled, and believes, from her conscience, that the said parties had then the carnal knowledge of each other.

Mrs. Errington, it must be admitted, paid but little attention to her dinners, when matters of more consequence were transacting. We cannot absolutely say how she was engaged while the repast was cooling, but we can give a shrewd conjecture ; and Molly Mitchell appears to favour our opinion. The Captain and she, it is supposed, were taking a wet and a relish together , or he might probably be instructing her in some new evolutions, with the modern methods of attack and defence. She is a woman who thirsted after knowledge, and if the Captain had any thing new to communicate, she was sure to pump him out of it. Polly Mitchell supposes the Captain discharged his musket, for, though she did not hear the report, she smelt the powder , and Mrs. Errington appeared to have been very much heated in the engagement.

The dinner was now cool, and Mrs. Errington, it is presumed, was equally so ; for she sat down to table with as much indifference as if she was retiring to bed with her husband. She picked a bit of the wing of a capon, without the least appetite , though, but half an hour before, it is thought, she had a most voracious propensity.

Molly Mitchell relates yet another scene, which has not been deposed to by any of the other witnesses. She says, that she ' once attended Mrs. Errington to bathing, and, while she was in the bathing machine, with only her shift and petticoat on, she called to a gentleman, who was a stranger to this deponent, by the name of Love, and desired him to come in, which he did, and staid about a quarter of an hour in the machine with her, and her bosom all the while was quite exposed to his sight.'

The same witness corroborates the clipping scene, and that ' Mrs. Errington gave her and Phebe Lush some hair in a paper, and told them to keep it for her sake, and says, she believes Mrs. Errington cut off such hair from her private parts.

Private parts seems to be an improper term here, for what is meant to be understood by it ! for, from the immense business, which appears to have been transacted there, Molly Mitchell would have expressed herself with more propriety, if she had called them her ' public parts.' But, perhaps, Polly is not censurable in this respect, as the reft of the witneffes make ufe of the fame expreffion. The term, is probably technical, in Doctors Commons, and frequently occurs in their learned and elaborate difquifitions It is a fubject often handled by the profeffors of ecclefiaftical law, and every proctor is fo well acquainted with it, that (to ufe a figurative expreffion) it is a bufinefs that he has at his 'fingers ends'

Towards the conclufion of Mary Mitchell's evidence fhe fays, with great gravity, 'that fhe thinks Mrs Errington did not behave in a fober, decent, modeft manner.

Mr. Thomas Branfton, of Lyme-Regis, gentleman, depofed nothing that has not been already mentioned But among other things, he fays, that, 'as far as fell under his obfervation, Mr Errington behaved to his wife with great tendernefs and affection, in every refpect, as a good hufband.'

James Baxter, another witnefs, fays, 'he was watchman and attendant on the officers on guard at the Bank of England, in the riots in June, 1780, and ftill continues in the fame fituation ; that Captain Buckley, of the Coldftream regiment of guards, ufed occafionally to do duty there, and that Mrs Errington, towards the latter end of the year 1781, frequently vifited him when on duty, and laid with him all night in one and the fame bed.'

Captain Buckley, it appears by this, had double duty to perform, and he fuppofed he was as fafe as the Bank from difcovery, but mafter James Baxter, who had been engaged by the city to prevent riots, could not endure fuch riotous proceedings He thought it an abominable offence, that people who were not free of the city, fhould come within the centre of its walls, to commit the foul crime of adultery. Had any one of the aldermen or common council thought proper to amufe himfelf with a lady on his premifes, he would, perhaps, like a good citizen, have winked at it, but for people to bring their harlots from the Weftminfter end of the town, to defile the more pure city of London, was a matter which his confcience would not permit him to conceal from the community.

Another witness, named Samuel Organ, who is a waiter at Mr. Ofbourne's hotel, in the Adelphi, fays, that ' Mr. and Mrs. Errington, at one time, lived in a houfe oppofite to his mafter's, that at firft, from the loofe manner of Mrs Errington's behaviour, he concluded fhe was not a married, but a kept woman, that he has frequently feen her ftanding at her chamber-window, dreffed very loofely, and her bofom all expofed, and, from the front window of her houfe, he has frequently feen her making figns to gentlemen who have happened to be at the faid hotel, that her behaviour at the window, was in general fo very immodeft, that his mafter and miftrefs often complained of it to gentlemen who came to their houfe, and hoped they would not take any notice of her '

Mrs Errington had no very particular attachments, but was equally hofpitable to all mankind. If bufinefs was but done, fhe little regarded by whom it was performed; a new morfel now and then, from the Hotel, muft have been an excellent repaft for her, and fhe never thought it any indelicacy to communicate her defigns, whether by geftures, words, or motions.

Edward Palmer, another waiter at Ofbourne's hotel, fays, ' he has often feen Mrs Errington half naked at her chamber window, and feen her throw herfelf into a variety of indecent poftures, and has frequently been called by gentlemen, who have been at his mafter's houfe, to come and look at her '

He alfo depofes that he delivered a letter to her, from a gentleman, which fhe read, and afterwards defired to fee the gentleman, and that fuch gentleman went to her houfe accordingly. He adds, that when Mrs. Errington was throwing herfelf into indecent poftures, he once faw her naked thighs '

Such are the leading features of the trial of Mrs Harriot Errington, and fuch are the obfervations which have occurred

The celebrated heroine of the preceding paper, whofe maiden name was H———t C———n, difcovered in her early days a violent predilection for gallantry. Her remarkable fprightlinefs and vivacity, led her on to romping with the boys at the boarding-school, to whom she found means of access, and notwithstanding all the care of her friends, and the vigilance of her guardian, she had like to have over-leaped all bounds, by taking a trip to Gretna-Green, before she was well entered into her teens.

At the age of fifteen, Miss Harriot set her tender heart on a promising youth, and shewed much emotion and sensibility on occasion of his death, which was by bathing in the Thames

In her sixteenth year, the most heedless spectator might have run and read the language of her susceptible soul, in her sparkling eyes, comely smiles, and high heaving bosom The fragrance of spring was not so delightfull as her breath; the roses of summer bloomed in her cheeks She arose to perfection, attracted the eyes of the gay and wanton youths; and grew the envy of her sex. At nineteen, the fair one anticipated the springing pleasures of the distant day, and longed to peep into the page of futurity.

Accordingly, Miss Harriot, accompanied by her maid, visited the gypsies of Norwood, and received from those pretenders to sooth-saying, certain dark predictions which highly pleased her fond imagination, beholding a representation of those scenes in which she was to act a capital part

It is said, that these false augurs presented Miss a spouse whose air and address but ill accorded with her warm wishes, because he appeared employed chiefly in in disputing with the parson about tythes, and engaged in a study rather too dry for a lady of her vigorous and volatile deportment

As in a mirror, Miss saw the day dawning, wherein her pleasures were to begin. All her future favours were set before her sight, just as they afterwards actually appeared. The Curate, Post-master, Captains, Footmen, Butler, Baker, and an uncounted croud of fine fellows passed on in procession, in the manner of the kings in Macbeth. Those who believe in predestination, will easily make an apology for the misconduct of our fair inconftant; for furely a poor weak woman can never be fuppofed capable of thwarting the decrees of fate itfelf, and thofe who caft the greateft weight into the fcale of free-will, muft reflect on the many temptations which urged her on to deviate from the thorny paths of virtue and tread the more foft and flowery ones of pleafure

Mifs Harriot, in due time beftowed her gentle hand on Mr. Errington, and made him happy in her charms, in time fhe produced a pledge of their mutual love, or, to ufe the language of the law, 'They lived and cohabited together, bed and board, as hufband and wife, and con-fummated their marriage by the pro-creation of children' So truly loving were they in their lives, during the firft twelve-months, that they might with a great degree of propriety have demanded the flitch of bacon at Dunmow. Happy, they dwelt on the banks of the filver Thames, in the pleafant village of Batterfea, and in that Elyfium, might have long enjoyed the pureft pleafures, without a mixture of alloy, had not an infinuating ferpent entered their paradife, and by his cunning, feduced this daughter of Eve, to tafte the forbidden fruit, that grew in the ' middle' of the garden

The firft tempter fhall be namelefs, becaufe he is not blazoned on the Bifhop's Book of Adultery, although he was the firft who cracked the commandment with our fair but frail fpoufe His tongue was more infinuating than oil, and his gnomon of a marvellous projection. His fhoulders were broad, his limbs ftout as thofe of Hercules: in fine, his make was mafculine throughout, and not a mite of the maccaroni was blended in his ath-letic frame. The man who charged his back with the gates of Gaza, was not much ftronger, when he lay in the lap of Dalilah

He foon enflamed the heart of the lady, attracted her ear to his tale, and pointed out all the W——s of an-tiquity, and the Adulterefles of his own day, as examples for the fair one to follow. He gained his point. Mrs. Errington yielded, and fo purfued the road to pleafure, or rather to difgrace, from which fhe could never after recede.

The Trial of Elizabeth Levering, Wife of W. Levering, of Gun-street, Spital Fields, Carpenter, for Adultery with Gideon Ginchenet, an Apprentice and Journeyman, and Charles Sadler; in the Confiftory Court of London, in May, 1792.

JOSEPH LEVERING, who worked, lodged, and boarded with his brother, fubftantiated the marriage, and faid, that Elizabeth Levering was a perfon of a very loofe life, and of a very abandoned, wicked, luftful, and profligate difpofition. He alfo witneffed as a perfon prefent, to the articles of feparation drawn up in the prefence of two attornies.

With all the reft of the witneffes, he affirmed, that Mrs. Levering ufed frequently to call Gideon Ginchenet out of the work-fhop, and detain him for hours together; this was fo frequent in Mr. Levering's abfence, that on fuch occafions, the notice of the reft of the men was fo much attracted, that they ufed frequently to fay, " Come Gideon, your miftrefs wants you; fhe cannot do without you."

John Healy an apprentice to Mr. Levering, faid, that his miftrefs would frequently hurry him and another to bed, faying Ginchenet fhould follow immediately; but which hardly ever occurred while they kept awake.—He had alfo feen them playing together in a manner that fhewed an uncommon degree of intimacy; and in particular he had feen Ginchenet take hold of his miftrefs's hand in the kitchen and kifs it, fhe at the fame time fuffer-

ing him to pull her about without finding the least
fault with him—she at other times pulling his hair
and slapping his face.   One night in particular, he
remembered, that Mrs. Levering came into their
bed-room with a candle in her hand, when Ginchenet
got up in his shirt and followed her; and this witness
afterwards putting on his breeches, followed him into
the kitchen, where he found Mrs. Levering, her
daughter, and another little girl, but did not observe
any indecent familiarities between the parties at
that time; on the contrary, Mrs. Levering affected
to complain of Ginchenet's appearing before her in
that manner: her daughter cried at the same time.

Another night, being in bed with Ginchenet,
Mrs. Levering came into the room, and pulled the
cloaths nearly off the former—Ginchenet then said,
he would not go: on which she left the room, and
began crying as soon as she got to the door, saying,
he would repent it.—Yet, before she went away,
she pulled the bed-cloaths off a second time, as low
as their knees.   It seems, that Healy being awake
when she first entered the room, he observed the
shadow of her fingers against the wall, beckoning
Ginchenet to follow her, which he was at first de-
determined to take no notice of.

Fanny Pounsford, wife of John Pounsford, one of
Mr. Levering's journeymen, used to attend Mr.
Levering's children, at his house in Gun-street,
Spital-fields; she said, Mrs. Levering was an abandoned woman—she knowing them several years,
had observed Mrs. Levering take great liberties
with Ginchenet, while an apprentice, having him
to dine, drink tea, and sup with her in Mr. Levering's absence; besides calling him out of the shop
at other times, to treat him with hot wine and
other liquors, indulging him with getting him what
he liked to eat—he, in return, used to bring home
tarts, &c. to treat his mistress.—And as a proof of
Mrs. Levering's insatiable disposition, she affirmed,

that she had known her call Ginchenet ten times a
day out of the shop from his work, she had likewise
seen him kiss her hand, and call her a pretty
woman; at other times, he has attempted to take
money out of her pocket, and on her hindering him,
he has called her a shabby creature to her face, and
the like.

Jane Hill, servant to Mr. Levering, went over
the same evidence, adding, that she heard her mistress say in Ginchenet's presence, that she loved him
and hated her husband; and that they were almost
always playing together: and in fine, that one night
in Mr. Levering's absence, going into her mistress's
room unawares, she heard them in bed together. And
that another time, Mr. Levering coming home rather
unexpectedly, Ginchenet was in his wife's bed room,
when he knocked at the door, and had much difficulty to get into his own apartment in his shirt, before Mr. Levering was let in.

Lucy Coleman another servant, testified, that Mrs.
Levering was loose in her manners; and that she
owned to her, that she doated on Ginchenet, and
loved the ground he walked upon, and could live
happier with him on a crust of bread, than with
her husband upon thousands.

Lucy Coleman further deposed, that one night
when Gideon Ginchenet had come home from a
journey, very much fatigued and gone to bed, she
was sent out about eleven o'clock, for some beer,
by her mistress, who ordered her not to knock at
the street door on her return, as she would wait for
her and let her in; that on her return she was much
surprised on finding no person at the door, and more
so on seeing a light in the counting-house that was
very near the passage, towards which she saw a man,
whom, at first, she supposed to be a robber, till seeing him feel her mistress's breasts, and kiss her, she
heard her say, "Don't Sadler! don't you see the
girl?" They then went up stairs, and the girl followed them towards the kitchen that was on the

same floor; Mrs. Levering then asked him if he would have any supper, to which he replied, No; but said he would drink some small beer—they then staid in the kitchen half an hour, taking the same liberties as before; but as the man asked her mistress to let him look at some needle-work in the dining-room, they both went in there, where they again kissed one another: and as the witness found the door was open, and thought they did not hear her, she looked into the room, and plainly saw them standing close together near the fire-place, Mr. Sadler with his back towards her, with his breeches quite hanging down, his hands round her mistress's waist, and his head at the same time inclined upon her bosom, while she leaned her head upon his shoulders; she at the same time saw her cloaths so far drawn up, as to discover part of her belly, and one of her thighs quite naked; but was prevented from making further observations, by supposing she heard something upon the stairs.

In this deposition, she had no doubt, but that the parties were then in the act of adultery together; neither were her suspicions that she heard somebody upon the stairs unfounded, for she had not been long in the kitchen, before she heard Mr. Levering call out and say, " I'll shoot you, Sadler! I'll enter an action against you to-morrow." Mr. Sadler immemediately ran down stairs, and Mr. Levering after him; but the other having shut the street-door, he followed Mrs. Levering into the kitchen, struck her, and said he would shoot her.

Besides this, being determined she should stay no longer in his house, he sent for two watchman; but as they refused to take charge of her, she slept with her maid that night, and went away to her brother's the next day.

This witness further proved, that she brought a letter from Mrs. Levering, to Gideon Ginchenet, after this separation, which was opened by her husband.

Mrs. Levering, it feems, had four children by her hufband; and feems to have had the culpability of her conduct increafed fo much the more, as her hufband was of a temper the moft kind and indulgent.—There is hardly a doubt, from what may be collected from this trial, but that from her importunity with Ginchenet, and her publicity with Sadler, that fhe was in a very ftriking degree a Mrs. Errington in miniature.

A fentence from bed, board, and mutual cohabition, was obtained in the ufual way.

Trial of John Curtis, a Publican, in Bifhopfgate-ftreet, London, for a Rape upon Sarah Tipple, Spinfter, during the Old Bailey Seffions, in February, 1793.

The witneffes being examined feparate, and Sarah Tipple Sworn, fhe faid—I am a fingle woman, I go to fervice; at the time of this affault I lived fervant with Mr. Curtis; and I am nineteen next Auguft.

I went to my place to Mr. Curtis's on Monday, this affair happened on Tuefday. I was up three pair of ftairs making of the beds, and my mafter came up ftairs and bolted the door; he infifted violence upon me immediately.

Q. You muft explain—He entered my body; he took and threw me on to the bed, and I called for affiftance; I fhrieked but once, and he put his hand and crammed the fheets into my mouth: as foon as he came into the room he bolted the door, he never spoke to me at all; he threw me on the bed without speaking to me; he put his private parts into mine.

Q. What passed then, did you make any resistance?—Yes.

Q. How did he manage to keep you down on the bed! did you resist?—He forced me down, and he laid on me in such a manner, that I could not get away.

Q. Had you stays on? I had a pair of stays on.

Q. Did you make all the resistance in your power? consider one hand was engaged at your mouth? I resisted as much as I could.

Q. Did you try to do him any injury?—Yes, all that lay in my power. I could not get away at any rate in the world.

Q. What past after he put his private parts into yours? How long might he be in that situation? How did he force himself on you? Did you see him take down his breeches?—He did that after he put his hand to my mouth, and then he forced his private parts into mine, and something warm came from him.

Q. During this time could not you make any resistance?—He put the sheet into my mouth, and I could not; I had done all that lay in my power.

Q. How long do you conceive he remained in that situation on your body?—Five minutes. After this was over he went out immediately and went and brought up some water, I was almost dead, and he brought up some water for me to drink, as I had fainted.

Q. What was your complaint?—I felt myself so ill I could not get up; I was there about three weeks afterwards; I did not know a soul in the world in London.

Q. When you did get up, whom did you find in the house?—I did not get up for about two hours;

my mafter was in the houfe, and the other partner too; there was a good many people in the tap-room, but I did not know them. There is a woman that lives up one pair of ftairs, but I did not know her at that time.

Q. When was it after this happened to you that you firft made any complaint?—I found myfelf very bad indeed, and I thought it might be becaufe I had never known any body before; at laft I applied to a furgeon.

Q. Did you not complain to your mafter of this ill-treatment?—No, I did not at all. But I went to the Three-Mitre court, in Fenchurch-ftreet, I would not ftay; after I found I had the bad diforder I afked the prifoner, my mafter, to get me into the hofpital, and he fent a conftable to take me up. I had left him a long time before I found out that it was fo; about nine weeks.

Q. Did you tell him he had committed a rape on you?—I did not know any thing about committing a rape; all I afked of him was to get me into the hofpital.

Q. Will you fwear upon your oath that you have never known him but that one time?—I never had any connection with him but then: he fent for a conftable and took me up; he faid I infulted him for money, but I did not.

Q. What anfwer did he make to that?—I did not hear him fay fo, the conftable told me fo; the conftable came and told me I muft go along with him, and he took me to the Compter.

Mr. *Knowlys.* Now my girl tell us a little more about this: There was a man of the name of Potts that lodged in the houfe?—There was.

Q. Did not the other two fervants fay, you was very fond of Potts.—They did fay fo.

Q. Did not Hannah, one of them, fay you fome-times got out of bed and cuddled Potts. Young woman was not you turned out of doors for being found in bed with Potts?—I was not.

Q. And so your master came in and never said a word to you, good, bad, or indifferent, never called you my dear; never courted you at all?—Never said a word, but immediately threw me down on the bed.

Q. You had never known any thing of this sort before?—Never before in my life.

Q. Which part of the bed did you fall against?—It was the side of the bed near the foot, and my head towards the other side,

Q. When he threw you on the bed, I suppose you suspected his intention?—I did, and shrieked out.

Q. You never shrieked out more than once?—He put the sheet into my mouth, immediately crammed it in; the sheet was in my mouth all the time of the business, he was holding it down with his hand.

Q. Then he had only one hand at liberty, for one hand was constantly employed in keeping down the sheet in your mouth; that was so?—It was.

Q. How was your two hands employed against his one?—My two hands were behind me.

Q. Pray, who was it put your hands in that shape?—Seeing him bar the door, I was frightened, and I held my hands so.

Q. You suspected, when you saw him bar the door? I did not know what he was going to do, I thought he was going to kill me, or something, I cried out, and he immediately chucked me on the bed.

Q. Then he shoved you on the bed the moment that he barred the door; how far is the bed from the door?—It is close.

Q. Then you had time to make one cry and no more; how came your hands to fall behind you?—I cannot tell.

Q. That was rather odd, was not it; did you ever in your life when you fell, having your hands close by your side, had your hands behind you before ; how could they be twisted backwards by that fall ?—I cannot tell.

Q. Then they remained behind all the time ?—I could not get them away, I made all the resistance I could ; I could not get my hands away.

Q. They then remained pinioned like a fowl ?—Exactly so ; he prevented me, he lay on me.

Q. The man is not two or three ton weight ?—I made all the resistance I possibly could.

Q. How could he by laying on you prevent your drawing one hand from under you ?—I made all the resistance I could.

Q. Then you really could not get one hand from under your back ; that man is not a very fat man ?—The moment I saw him bar the door, the moment my strength failed me directly. I being in a strange place, what did I suppose that that man was going to do !

Q. Did you slap his face ?—I did not.

Q. Did you pull his hair ?—I could not get away.

Q. Did you kick him at all ?—I kicked him all that lay in my power.

Q. Then you almost overturned him by your kicking ?—I don't know, I cannot say but what I might.

Q. Here he lays on you, and you kicking about, it is natural you should almost overturn him ?—I did all that was in my power.

Q. Did you kick his shins, or did you not kick at all ?—I did all that lay in my power to get away. I tried to get up.

Q. How did you try to get up; the moment that you fell down, he threw himself upon you ; where was your petticoats ?——He pulled up my petticoats.

Q. Were they pulled up before you was on the bed, or after ? ——After.

Q. How did he manage with his other hand ?—And then he laid his knee on me, and in that situation he lay on me ; he kept my petticoats high up with his knee.

Q. And in that situation he did it ?—No, he did not do it so.

Q. What did he do with his knee ?—After he pulled up my petticoats he laid his knee on me to keep them up while he pulled down his breeches.

Q. He continued his knee there then ?—No, he did not.

Q. What kept your coats up ?—He took his knee up when he unbuttoned his breeches ; he was on the bed, and my coats kept up.

Q. Did they keep up of their own accord, or did you keep them up ?—He kept them up, to be sure.

Q. Now, how did he keep them up ?—he had not three hands, had he ?—No.

Q. Now, let us dispose of the two ; how did he keep them up ?—I cannot tell.

Q. How high were your clothes ?—My clothes were quite up to my chin.

Q. And you struggled and kicked about a good deal, did not you ?—All that lay in my power.

Q. Still they kept up to your chin ; you was quite a maid at this time ?—I never knew a man before.

Q. Will you tell us how he managed to bring his private parts to your's ? can you say how he did that ?—No.

Q. Did you cross your legs ?—No.

Q. It did not occur to you that that would be a good way to stop him ; did you keep your legs a little wider than usual ?—I don't know that I did.

Q. Don't you know that you did not ?—I don't know that I did not.

Q. I should have thought keeping the legs close

would be the best way to prevent him ; do you know how he managed to introduce his private parts ? where was the hand that was at liberty ? one hand was at the 'sheet at your mouth, where was the other hand ?—I cannot tell.

Q. Cannot you tell me how he managed to introduce his private parts to you, because you know you was a maid ?—No.

Q. Nor where his hand was ? was it employed to prevent your struggling ?—He laid on me.

Q. Really, my girl, in the way you describe it, I cannot see how such a thing could be effected ?—He certainly did.

Q. You did not feel where the other hand was ; you never felt how he employed the other hand ? —No.

Q. Never felt it about your person at all ?— Yes.

Q. Then how was it employed ?—He took his other hand to put his private parts into mine.

Q. Now, my girl, how came you to tell me, a minute ago, that you did not know how it was employed, because I put it to you several times ?— Because I was ashamed.

Q. When one hand was on your mouth, and the other hand was so employed, a very little struggle would have put him off ; how came it you did not get rid of him when both hands were engaged ? —I did all in my power.

Q. Did he continue this hand to his private parts all the time that he did this to you ?—No, not all the time.

Q. How did he employ it afterwards ?—I cannot tell you, I am sure.

Q. How came you to tell nobody of this affair ? —I had no friends nor any acquaintance in London or else I would have told them.

Q. Did you complain to your fellow-servant of

your parts being fore?—No, not at all; neither did I shew them to any body.

Robert Carrol sworn. I am a silk weaver; I never saw the girl, only by bringing beer to my house from Mr. Curtis: he lives next door; she left her place, and she brought her box, and she asked my wife to wash her some linen, and she did; this was within a week or a fortnight after she left her place, I cannot say nearer; she told my wife she was going to live at No. 88, Houndsditch. Several weeks after she came back again to my house, and slept there; when I perceived she walked lame, and my wife used to tell me she washed herself with fuller's earth, and said, she was chafed. I said to her, if you have any thing a matter with you, I will go with you to a surgeon: I did so, and the surgeon examined her, and said, he thought there was nothing a matter, without her blood was bad; and then she came back again, and got worse and worse: I asked her several times if she was ever acquainted with her master; I meant joking among ourselves; it was said, that Mr. Curtis was rather fond of a woman; it was not done out of any harm to Mr. Curtis: she said, that her master never offered any thing to her, that he never behaved any way ill to her: but about a month after this, she came up to my loom-side, and said, My master Curtis gave me the bad distemper! I asked her how she knew it? She told me that he was obliged to take the plaisters off before he could meddle with her.

Q. How often did she pretend that he had meddled with her?—I cannot say.

Q. Did you understand from this language, that he had meddled with her more than once?—I should imagine by that, that he did; I asked her, Did you ever tell your master that he gave you this distemper? She said No. I asked her two or three times over, she said No, she never told him or her mistress of it. She then begged of me to ask her master to get her into an hospital to get cured; I told her no, I could not think of doing of any such thing, for the time was so long, I could not think of troubling my head about the matter; and if she had any thing to say to him, they must decide it themselves. She told me that she had a sister at the other end of the town.

Court. Just now she swore that she did not tell this to any body, because she had not a friend in town.

Here the examinations ended; and the Court, as it might naturally be expected, found the prisoner Not Guilty.——This trial, upon the whole, affords a striking lesson upon the depravity of principles among the females of the lower order, especially when sharpened by resentment or neglect; but, thanks to the mildness of the British laws, and the scrutinizing powers of an unbiassed Judge and Jury, cases of life and death are not determined upon at random.

The Case of John Bury, Esq. of the County of Devon, who was divorced for want of his Testicles. Tried in 1561.

JOHN BURY, Esq was a man of considerable landed estate, which principally lay in the county of Devon, where he resided. Being at length tired of a single life, he resolved to enter on the holy state of matrimony; and for this purpose, paid his addresses, and shortly after married, one Willimot Gifford, of the same county; a lady

poffeffing many perfonal charms. The marriage took
place the 20th of November, in the firft year of Queen
Mary.

The bride, who felt all the force of nature, was much
furprized when the next morning came, to find that her
hufband had rifen, and that nothing of a very tender concern
had occurred but fhe concluded, that his extreme refpect for her had prevented him from taking the laft liberty
in a precipitate manner, and confoled herfelf, that fhe was
to be initiated into the myfteries of Hymen by degrees.
The next night, however, proved equally, if not more,
unfatisfactory as the former, for the round-a-bout en-
dearments which he beftowed, only made her the more
defirous of an inftant explanation. Delicacy forbade
her to point the way, or certain it is, that fhe would
have compelled him to difcharge the duties of his ftation.
Days, and weeks, and months and years, paffed on juft in
the fame manner, they went to bed to repofe, and rofe
again to follow the bufinefs, or the pleafures of the day.
Let us for a moment pity a blooming young lady, in the
height of blood and vigour, married to a man who could
not deprive her of that virgin mark which fhe had pre-
ferved with much care, for heightening his opinion, and
for adding to the common ftock of love and while we
commiferate, let us not blame her for communicating
her deplorable fituation to a female confidant. This
confidant was a mother, who defcribed to her all the pro-
cefs of the tender communication between man and
wife • now were the eyes of poor Willimot opened, her
indignation was juftly raifed, and fhe very properly determined to call her un-family hufband before the Ecclefiaftical Judge, charging him to be ' impotentem ad
coeundum cum dicta Willimote, propter vitium perpe-
tuum, & incurabile impendimentum ad generationem, &
ejus inhabilitatem,' and therefore defiring to be divorced.

In fupport of this charge, feveral witneffes were called, two of whom were phyficians : thefe unravelled the
whole myftery, by declaring, that the faid J. Bury, Efq,

had but one little stone about the size of a bean In further proof it was asserted by several experienced matrons, that Willimot was at that time a virgin, in the strict sense of the word. These facts were of so strong a nature, that Bury, at length, made a full confession, on which the Judge pronounced a sentence of divorce.

But what most astonished us—and, what no doubt, will most astonish our readers—was, the circumstance that this impotent man should, some short time afterwards, marry another woman called Philip Monjoy. and that she should be delivered of a son by him! Perhaps this event savours as strongly of Cuckoldom, as any other in the annals of gallantry for, notwithstanding this auspicious birth. we find an interruption of matrimonial joys occurred in a short space of time, Mrs. Monjoy, without appealing to the laws—perhaps she could not go into Court with clean hands—precipitately left her husband, and married a Mr. Langeden, with whom she ever after continued.

It is, therefore, perhaps, not unreasonable to conclude that Bury had been cornuted by Langeden, to whom the birth of the son may be attributed In Bury's doleful situation, he no doubt considered the affair as a piece of friendship and, on the other hand, if he took the atchievement to himself, it must wonderfully have contributed to the good gentleman's peace of mind for though on his examination at the suit of his first wife, he acknowledged that she was a virgin, for aught he knew to the contrary ; it is not impossible but the Graham or the Forman of that day, might have fleeced his purse, on the pretence of removing his unfortunate defect.

Trial of the Right Hon. Lady Ann Foley, Wife of the Hon. Edward Foley, Esq. and Daughter of William Earl of Coventry, for Adultery with the Right Hon. Charles Henry Earl of Peterborough, in the Consistorial and Episcopal Court at Doctor's Commons.

ANOTHER instance of licentious wickedness, and infamous indifference to public opinion, almost surpassing any preceding relation, in scandalous and bare-faced defiance of every sentiment of decency!

The Libel exhibited before the Episcopal Court, stated the marriage of the Hon Edward Foley, and the Right Hon. Lady Ann Foley, the then Right Hon. Laday Ann Coventry, on the 24th of October, 1778: the necessary documents were produced and properly authenticated. Mr. Foley and his Lady, lived together with every affection on his part, and were commonly reputed, taken, and acknowledged to be man and wife by their relations, neighbours, and acquaintance; about the latter end of the month of November, 1783, Lady Foley set out for London, and went to the house of Miss Foley, in Chandos-street, to make preparations for a journey to the Continent; and Mr Foley intended to follow her to London, but having been informed that a criminal intimacy had subsisted and was subsisting between his wife and the Earl of Peterborough, he declined his intention, and immediately separated himself from union and company with Lady Foley.

It was some time in the year 1781, that Lord Deerhurst, brother to lady Foley, introduced the Earl of

Peterborough to the acquaintance and friendship, and into the house, of Mr Foley, and from that time a strong intimacy continued in or near the months of January, February, and March, 1782, whilst Mr. Foley resided in Weymouth-street, the Earl of Peterborough frequently paid morning visits to, and dined with, Mr. Foley and Lady Foley his wife, and was always entertained by Mr. Foley, in the most friendly and hospitable way about the month of April 178 , the Earl of Peterborough returned from the Continent, Mr. Foley then lived in Somerset-street, and his Lordship there renewed his intimacy and visits to Mr. Foley and his wife: the latter, in August 1783, came from Herefordshire to London, and went to live at the house of the Hon. Miss Foley in Chandos-street; here also they were frequently visited by the Earl of Peterborough. after this they went to Hastings, accompanied by Lord Peterborough, and from thence to Brighthelmstone, where his Lordship staid but one day: in November ensuing, Mr. Foley and Lady Foley returned to London, to a house in South-street, where his Lordship was very frequent in his attendance: about the latter end of April 1784, Lord Peterborough went to Cheltenham in Gloucestershire, for the benefit of his health, as he pretended, and from that place wrote to Mr. Foley, at Stoke Court, in Herefordshire, about 30 miles distant, enquiring after his and Lady Foley's health: and Mr Foley had not then the slightest suspicion that any thing criminal subsisted between lady Foley and him an invitation was shortly sent to his Lordship, to come and spend some time at Stoke Court, which invitation he accepted, and in May 1784, paid his first visit to Mr. Foley and Lady Foley at Stoke Court, and from that time until about the Second of September 1784, his Lordship several times visited them there for the course of a few days, and then returned to Cheltenham: about the second of September, he came back to Stoke Court, with his servants and horses, and continued entirely to reside there till about the 20th: Lord Peterborough having thus, by various acts, established an intimacy in Mr. Foley's family, and taken opportunity thereby to seduce the affections of Lady Foley from her husband, she being a woman of a profligate and adulterous disposition, they did mutually carry on a wicked and criminal correspondence, which continued to be a matter of great notoriety.

About the month of March 1784, Mr Foley and Lady Ann Foley his wife, went to a ball given by his Royal Highness the Prince of Wales, at Carleton House. Mr. Foley did not stay long at Carleton House, but retired and left Lady Foley there, who staid till about four or five the next morning, and then left Carleton House in Mr Foley's coach, accompanied by the Earl of Peterborough, and no person besides, his Lordship ordered the coachman, Thomas Simmonds, to drive to his Lordship's mother's house, in Dean-street, Soho, which he accordingly did; when they arrived there, the Earl of Peterborough ordered Thomas Andrews, the footman not to knock at the door, and Thomas Simmonds staid on the coach box; the blinds of the coach were drawn up, and they stopped in that situation about an hour   during that time the coachman and footman perceived the coach to be in motion several times, though the horses stood quite still; the coachman, as he sat on the box, looked through the front window of the coach, and the morning being remarkably fine, and the moon shining so clear as almost to equal the light of day, he plainly saw the Right Hon. Lady Ann Foley laying upon her back, upon the back seat of the said coach, with her naked thighs exposed, and Lord Peterborough laying upon her, and between her naked thighs, and they were then in the very act of carnal copulation; and the motion of the coach was occasioned thereby.

Frequently, at other times, in the winter of the year 1783, and the spring of the year 1784, Thomas Simmonds the coachman, hath, at nights, drove the Right Hon. Lady Ann Foley, and the Earl of Peterborough, in Mr. Foley's coach, about the streets of London, the coachman hath, by his Lordship's order, stopt many

times ; the blinds have been pulled up, and Lady Ann
and the Earl have had the carnal use and knowledge of
each others bodies, and committed the crime of Adultery · in May 1784, when his Lordship was at Mr Foley's house at Stoke Court. William Maull, master of
the Crown Inn, at Worcester, by order of Mr Foley,
sent his servant, Benjamin Smith, with a pair of job-
horses, for the use of his carriage , about three weeks after Benjamin Smith went to Stoke Court with the job-
horses, he drove Lady Foley and Lord Peterborough
alone together, in his Lordship's coach, about two miles
from Stoke Court, near Eastwood, in the turnpike road
to Sudbury , and as he was driving the carriage gently
up hill, he looked through the front window of the coach,
and plainly perceived Lady Foley laying on her back,
on the bench in the coach, with her thighs naked, (the
coach had a large double window in the front, and a narrow bench within, to communicate from one seat to the
other) and extended and exposed towards his sight, and
Lord Peterborough was then laying upon her, in the
very act of carnal copulation, and continued in that position several minutes, thus having the carnal use and
knowledge of each other's bodies, and committing the
crime of Adultery.   After his Lordship and Lady Ann
had left the coach, Benjamin Smith found, in one of the
pockets thereof, a white handkerchief, with several marks
or stains thereon, and which had been used by Lord Peterborough and Lady Foley, or by one of them, to
wipe their, or one of their private parts.

   Shortly after this occurrence, Benjamin Smith drove
Lady Ann and his Lordship in a phæton, to the top of
Stoke Park, near the double gates there, where Lord
Peterborough ordered him to stop; getting out of the
phæton, his Lordship proposed a walk to Lady Ann,
upon which she left the carriage, and they walked together about fifty yards from the place where the carriage stood, and then Lady Ann laid herself down on
the grass near some gorse , his Lordship upon this directly unbuttoned his breeches, and pulled up her petti-

P

coats, and laid down upon her, and they had there the carnal use and knowledge of each other's bodies. they continued on the ground together about ten minutes, and, during that time, they were perceived by Benjamin Smith with the utmost clearness.

On the ensuing day, Benjamin Smith drove Lady Ann and the Earl, in the phaeton, to the top of Stoke Park, near the double gates there, and close to the spot they were at the day before, here he stopped by Lord Peterborough's orders, and Lady Ann and his Lordship descending from the phaeton, walked on together for the space of one hundred yards among the trees; there they stopped, and Lady Ann put her back to and leaned against an oak tree, and either she or Lord Peterborough pulled her petticoats up to her waist, and thereby exposed her naked thighs, his Lordship then pulled down his breeches and got between her legs and thighs, and then carnally enjoyed her there, leaning against the oak-tree, they had the carnal use and knowledge of each others bodies, and committed the foul crime of adultery, which fact was clearly seen by Benjamin Smith, and J. Hookey, Lord Peterborough's servant.

One day, some time between May and September 1784. Benjamin Smith drove Lady Ann and his Lordship in a phaeton, on the turnpike road from Stoke Court, to the city of Hereford, during the journey, he perceived Lady Ann with her petticoats up sitting in the said Lord Peterborough's lap, whose breeches were down and her hand therein, and on his Lordship observing that Benjamin Smith noticed it, he said, Postboy, mind your horses, and don't look at us!

On Friday the 9th of July 1784, Lady Ann Foley and Lord Peterborough had a meeting, and agreed to continue their criminal intimacy on the ensuing Sunday; the next Monday was the day fixed for the election of Members of Parliament, for the city of Hereford, and on Saturday the 10th, being the Saturday before the election Lord Peterborough sent a letter to Lady Ann Foley, intimating therein, that he had repented having appointed Sunday for their interview, that he thought Mr. Foley's arrival on the next day a certainty, as the Hereford election would be on Monday, that, his Lordship conceived, would be a more eligible day, as her Ladyship would be certain of Mr. Foley's absence, in conclusion, his Lordship named the three-mile stone from Ledbury, as the place, and Monday at half after five as the time of meeting.

On Thursday the 30th September, 1784, Lady Ann Foley and Lord Peterborough were together in a walk in the shrubbery, near the grotto, in Mr Foley's grounds, at Stoke Court, and his Lordship was standing with Lady Ann in his arms, her arms were round his neck, and her legs round his, with her cloaths up to her waist, and her nakedness exposed from the waist downwards, his arms were round her body, and both their bodies in motion, and they were then in the very act of carnal copulation, and then had the carnal use and knowledge of each other's bodies, and thereby committed the foul crime of adultery all this was plainly seen by John Davies, a a bricklayer, who had been that day employed in pulling down a pigeon-house in Stoke Park, and was returning from his work, and walking along the road, parellel with the said shrubbery, he heard Lady Ann Foley cry out three times, 'Oh dear," and say, 'you hurt me!' All this was a matter of public notoriety

Samuel Purlewent, of Lincoln's Inn, Gentleman, proved the marriage of the Hon Mr Foley and the Right Hon. Lady Ann. Foley. Mr Purlewent was employed as agent by Mr. Foley's attorney, Mr. White, and said, that in Hillary Term last, Edward Foley brought his action in his Majesty's Court of King's Bench at Westminster, against the Right Hon Charles Henry Earl of Peterborough and Monmouth, for damages sustained by reason of a criminal correspondence carried on by the Earl, with Lady Ann Foley, the wife of Edward Foley: in the month of March in the year 1785, the cause came on to be heard at the Assizes held at the city of Hereford, before Sir George Nares, Knt and Sir James Eyre, Knt and a Jury of lawful and honeſt men, duly impannelied and ſworn, at which Aſſizes the deponent was preſent; when the Jury having heard the evidence, brought in a verdict for the Hon Edward Foley, the plaintiff, with two thouſand five hundred pounds damages. Mr Purlevent alſo depoſed to the authenticity of a copy of the verdict exhibited, and alſo to the identity of the perſons of the Hon. Edward Foley, the Right Hon Lady Ann Foley, and Charles Henry Earl of Peterborough and Monmouth.

John Robinſon, of Bolton-ſtreet, Piccadilly, Gentleman, depoſed to the hand-writing of the Earl of Peterborough, what appears ſingular is, that this gentleman does not affix the ſignature of his name, but his mark to his depoſition.

This was the whole of the evidence adduced, upon the hearing of which the Court adjudged, that a definitive ſentence be promulgated; viz. it was therefore pronounced and decreed, that the Hon Edward Foley, Eſq. ſhould be divorced, &c from bed, board, and mutual cohabition with his wife, by reaſon of Adultery by her committed

Surely the ſcandalous ſcenes here related, could not have been exceeded by any of the ſhocking enormities committed by the great and noble, during the licentious reign of our ſecond Charles! what an admirable ſcheme, on the return from Carlton Houſe, was that of Lord Peterborough's ordering the coach to proceed to his mother's houſe in Dean-ſtreet, and there to ſtand ſtill. while the amorous pair, ' hot with the Tuſcan grape, and high in blood,' (and inflamed her Ladyſhip perhaps had been by ſome liquor. during her ſtay at Carlton Houſe) enjoyed themſelves in ſoft dalliance it is curious to conſider the ſituation of the ſervants on the coach-box, their ſurpriſe on hearing his Lordſhip's order to let the coach *ſtand ſtill* in the ſtreet, they might poſſibly ſuppoſe it was their intention to *repoſe* ſome little ſpace in that ſituation the chuckling and grinning, and broken hints of thoſe candid interpreters of awkward ſituations, livery servants, may however, be easily guessed at, and then how must the philosophy of Thomas Simmonds, the coachman, have been puzzled, at seeing the coach move, while the horses stood perfectly still, till venturing to look through the window, he, assisted by the light of the moon, perceived that memorable scene so highly complimentary to the delicacy of modern manners, and so peculiarly honourable to the character of her Ladyship as a wife, and the feelings of his Lordship as a friend! How would the good old Lady have been affected, had she known the scene of wickedness her son was transacting at her door! Perhaps, she was at that very moment, offering some prayer for strengthening the religious and moral principles of his Lordship!

These scenes, it appeared, frequently occurred in the streets of London, and they seem freaks of the imagination, this amiable couple must have been very partial to: but the country was a place more adapted to this mode of indulgence, in bye-roads, &c the favourite propensity might be humoured, without much hazard of detection, except from the curiosity of the driver, which was an evil to be feared alike in every place, thus driving gently up hill near Sudbury, the postillion perceived them in the last exposure of shameless guilt, nor must the scenes where Lady Ann reclines herself on the grass, or leans herself back against the oak-tree, be left unnoticed, though fit only to grace the annals of vulgar prostitution. These circumstances according to the evidence of the postillion, happened about the month of May, the Spectator somewhere, advises his fair readers against too great an intimacy with Sylvan scenes in that month, but had the high-bred dames of fashion, of that period, even degraded themselves by obscenities like those we have been obliged to relate, that censor of the public morals would, perhaps, almost have despaired of the efficacy of precept, and have vented his sentiments only, in indignant exclamation, or contemptuous sarcasm

What must her Ladyship's feelings and sentiments have been, when his Lordship admonished the postillion, on his looking at them, to mind his horfes, and not the employment of the company he was driving! O virtuous education, pride of birth, female dignity and delicacy, how were ye all degraded, loft! the meaneft wretch could not have ftooped to lower infamy. Imperial Rome we will no longer furvey as prodigies, thy Agrippina's, Meffalina's, &c. England can vie with thee in fome of thy moft profligate exhibitions of moral evil.

The occurrences of this Trial, indeed, only take the lead of numberlefs others of equal atrocity, fome more heightened by wantonnefs, and more caricatured by burlefque: the utmoft impartiality, the ftricteft adherence to truth, will be obferved in every narration; no favour will be allowed to rank or influence, nor will an already degraded name be crufhed by unmerited obloquy. as our materials are drawn from the moft authentic fources our means of information are unbounded, it is to the public we write, and, therefore, truth and candour will ever be the grand directors of our compofitions.

The celebrated Cafe and Trial of the Marquis de Gefvres, upon the complaint of his Lady, Mademoifelle de Mafcranny, who, after three years Marriage, commenced a Suit againft him, at Paris, for Imbecility and Impotency.

THOUGH in point of morality and prudence, fome people might think cafes of this kind better concealed than difplayed, the contrary is the fact, and further, the publication of fuch criminality as is generally the caufe of them, is loudly demanded by the united voices of justice and humanity *

To place these assertions in a clear, and indubitable light, only let it be considered, to what trials the modesty of a woman is exposed, if united to a sham husband!—What cruel assaults and experiments has she not to sustain! The image of such a husband, lifeless as it is, cannot but kindle some kind of desire, yet, like the apples of Tantalus, it can only torment.—And, as it is notorious, that the rage of a fumbler, is apt to hurry him into extravagancies, and even revenge, the life of a woman, hampered with such a one, may be highly endangered.—These imperfect men always seek to do away their own shame by criminating somebody else! There is a remarkable instance of this in the conduct of a King of Castile. But to return; all the while the connection of the parties in question, endured, it was pleaded by the lady's advocate, that her husband wanted little else but power to perform his duty, always imitating, even the gestures, kind looks, postures, and in fine every thing but reality, so that there was not only a cohabitation, a condormetion, viz a sleeping together, but also offers and essays of consummation, all in vain and without effect. The first legal step taken in this business, was to have a form of interrogation drawn up (and this was partly done by the commands of the lady's confessors) The lady in her charge, does not tax her husband with the want of the organs necessary for generation, but only urges, that these organs are absolutely destitute of motion. This kind of imbecility, is what the Canons call frigidity.

When the Marquis was interrogated by the proper officers, he readily answered every question but that, ask-

* This case is illustrated by a number of parallel cases, ancient and modern, confirmed by Ecclesiastical Decrees, the Judgment of the Canonists, Civilians, and Common Lawyers, and is translated purposely for this work, from the French original, together with an English version of all the particular passages, that have hitherto appeared in Latin only.

ing him, whether he had confummated his marriage? For this he demanded three days to make his reply, not withftanding it was expreffed in the brief, put into the hands of his counfel, that he had confummated it feven or eight hundred times!

The form of the Interrogations are as follow:

Interrogatory made by us Anthony Dorfanne, &c. official of Paris, by virtue of a Sentence of the 16th Inftant, at the requeft of Mademoifelle Mary-Magdalen Emilia de Mafcranny, affifted as much as is requifite by Madame de Caumartin, and the Sieur Abbot de Mafcranny, her guardians ad hoc, plaintiff. April, 1712.

I. Concerning his name, furname, age, quality, and habitation, after having taken an oath to deliver the truth?

Says, his name is Joachim-Bernard Potior, Chevalier, Marquis de Gefvres, &c. aged nineteen years and a half, living in the Street St Auguftin, in the parifh of St Roch.

II. Being afked, whether, fince his marriage, he had done as much as in him lay to arrive at the end of the faid marriage, and whether he had confummated it?

Said he had.

III. Whether it be not true, that finding himfelf unable to confummate the marriage, he fpent the firft night in complimenting his wife, without going about to confummate it, giving her to underftand he was very much incommoded in his ftomach, by having eaten part of an eel pye.

Said, that finding himfelf very much out of order with a ficknefs at his ftomach, occafioned by having eaten part of an eel pye, he did not confummate the marriage that night.

IV. Whether he does not know that his valet de chambre, who, undoubtedly, was fome how informed, that he was unable to confummate the marriage, faid the next day to one of the chambermaids of Mademoifelle de

Mafcranny, that he d d not think his mafter had confummated the marriage, becaufe he had heard fay, that
his c--dpiece was tied up, which is a fort of forcery ?

Anfwer, he knew nothing of it, and that he thought
it was forged.

V. Whether it be not true that, the next day after he
was married, being uneafy to find that he was unable to
confummate the marriage, he pretend d to be fick. and
the better to make Mademoifelle de Mafcranny believe
fo, affected, at his arrival at St Owen, whither they
went to fpend part of the day, to lie n the bed til eight
in the evening, when he rofe to a collation ?

Anfwer, faid it was true, that his illnefs continuing all
the next day after he was married, he was obliged, when
he arrived at St. Owen, to throw himfelf upon the bed.

VI. Whether it be not true, that returning to Paris
at ten o clock that night, he retired into his apartment,
where he lay alone, for fear that if he fhould lie with
Mademoifelle de Mafcranny, fhe fhould perceive that
his illnefs was feigned, and that to hinder her even from
enquiring into his health, he had the precaution not to
let her know that he would not lie with her

Said, it was true that his illnefs continuing, he made
Mademoifelle de Gefvres acquainted with it, and went
to lie in his own apartment

VII Whether, perceiving that Madame de Mafcranny did not know what was the duty of married people,
or the confummation of marriage, he did not turn her
ignorance to his own advantage. and fpent the following
nights, Monday and Tuefday, in making her new proteftations and compliments, and in embracing her amo-
roufly, without going about to confummate the marriage?

Said, the charge i falfe, and that he confummated the
marriage, Monday and Tuefday.

VIII. Whether, on his fetting out for the army, he
did not teftify all the tendernefs imaginable, to Mademoifelle de Mafcranny, and to give her more fenfible

marks of his friendship, writ to her during his absence, two or three times a day?

Said, that this article is true

IX Whether he does not know that the Duke de Tresmes, his father, went the next day after his departure, to wait upon Mademoiselle de Mascranny at her toilette, to inform himself about what had passed between them; but finding her little acquainted with such things, and thereby judging that she was not likely to complain of the condition of his son, who, he knew, was unable to consummate the marriage, he retired without giving her any information upon that head?

Said, he had no knowledge of the fact contained in that article, and that he had heard his father say, that it was false.

X. Whether the same Madame de Mascranny, being informed that the Marquis would very shortly arrive from the army, went to meet him, according to his request, and that being at Bourget, Madam de Revel, her aunt, did not take all opportunities of leaving them alone, thinking that in so doing, they obliged the Marquis, but, that then, there passed nothing particular between them, the latter contenting himself with making great shows of endearment?

Said, that article was true, and that there was nothing particular between him and Mademoiselle de Gesvres, because the place was not proper

XI. Whether, being arrived at Paris, he did not lay with her, and pass the night in caresses, and new demonstrations of fondness without going about to consummate the marriage?

Said, the charge was false, and that he rendered her the duty of marriage.

XII. Whether, during his stay at Paris, he did not lie four or five times a week with her, without having ever consummated the marriage, contenting himself with embracing her tenderly, and feeling her?

Said, that he had laid with her all that time, and that he often rendered her the duties of marriage.

XIII Whether one night in particular he did not take great care to wrap himself up in his shirt, and had the precaution to hold Madame de Mascranny by the hands, because she had writ him word, when he was at the army, she had been at the marriage of a lady of her acquaintance, who had taught her a great many things which before she was ignorant of?

Said, he had laid with her that night, and rendered her then the duties of marriage.

XIV. Whether, during the six months, whilst he staid at Paris, he could not consummate the marriage, though he often went about to do it, always giving over after having hugged and embraced his wife, and nothing else

Said it was false.

XV. Whether, when he went about to consummate the marriage, he did not feel great agitations, and that always finding himself unable to perform the action of marriage for want of erection, he gave over without doing any thing?

Said it was false, and that Mademoiselle de Gesvres, must needs remember to have often felt the effects of erection.

XVI Whether the Duke de Tresmes, well knowing that he was impotent, had not shown himself very much concerned at the want of consummation, and often discoursed with Madame de Mascranny upon that subject, and testified his uneasiness to his son, who being disturbed at it, had desired his wife not to speak any more of it to his father, to which she replied, that it was not she who spoke of it, but the Duke of Tresmes himself, who daily questioned her upon that article, and that he should desire him not to speak any more of it, for that she would not?

Said, he knew nothing of this article, and that he had only heard his father say, he had talked privately with the lady, but never concerning the impotence she complains of, being persuaded of the contrary.

XVII. Whether the said Sieur de Trefmes did often, in private, solicit him, the son, to do his endeavours to arrive at consummation, and did even desire Mademoiselle de Mafcranny to make some advances on her side, but that he tried in vain to arrive at consummation, finding himself in a natural impotence to do it?

Said, that the fact contained in this article is entirely false

XVIII. Whether the next morning, as he was going out of his chamber, Madam de Rafficod having asked him, if he had done his wife *well over*, after having been so long absent from her? he did not reply, Ask my valet de chambre, and he will tell you: and that the valet de chambre immediately said, that the Marquis had told him as a secret, that he had r....d the said Mademoiselle de Mafcranny seven times that night, though he did not so much as go about to consummate the marriage, being unable to do it, but only fondled and groped her as usual?

Said, the whole fact contained in this article was forged.

XIX. Whether, as he staid five or six days at Gesvres, at the time of that first journey, he did not lay every night with Mademoiselle de Mafcranny, without being ever able to consummate the marriage, and that for fear she should perceive his impotence he took great care to wrap himself up with two or three pairs of trowsers and breeches on at a time when he was up, and when he was with her in bed he did the same with his shirt, always taking the said Mademoiselle de Mafcranny fast hold by the hands?

Said, no; and that as for the latter part of it, he never wrapped himself up with trowsers, or with his shirt, and that it is a fictitious story

XX. Whether he had not formerly a rupture, with which he was very much incommoded, and was in the hands of a surgeon of Paris, and afterwards in those of a woman, who applied plaisters to his natural parts, in order to cure him of that rupture?

Said, that he had once a rupture, of which he was

cured, and that at present he suffered no inconveniency upon that account, that having had the said rupture at the age of two years, and that he had been told that he never had any plæsters applied to his natural parts

XXI Whether since he was in the hands of that woman he has felt no ail in his natural parts, that might hinder their functions, or at least, whether he has no remains of it?

Said, that he never felt any ail, as he answered to the preceding article

XXII Whether the plaisters of a woman who had him in hand, being in all likelihood composed of astringent medicines, to retain the parts which caused the opening in the rupture, did not affect the testicles, and shrink up the nerves which served for erection of the penis—so that he was no longer capable of erection?

Said the charge was false

XXIII. Whether he would consent to have the said Mademoiselle de Mascranny visited, in order to justify what he advances, and to put a stop to the report of her being still a virgin?

Said, that the proposal was so contrary to decency and modesty, that he need make no answer to it.

XXIV. Whether his reasons to hinder Mademoiselle de Mascranny from being visited, are only specious pretences which he used to conceal the truth of the marriage not being consummated?

Said, no, he having consummated the said marriage.

Interrogatories put to Mademoiselle de Mascranny.

I. Being asked concerning her name, sur-name, age, quality, and habitation, after having taken an oath to deliver nothing but truth—

She said, her name is Mary Magdalen Emilia de Mascranny, daughter of Messire Bartholomew Mascranny, master of requests of the Hostel du Roy, aged twenty years and a half, living at the Religieuses of Calvary, in the street of Vautgerrard.

II. Whether it was not at the perfuafion of perfons of ill difpofitions, and who are enemies to the family of the faid Marquis de Gefvres, that fhe engaged in the accufation of impotency, which fhe has entered againft him?

Said, that fhe did not do it at the perfuafion of any body, but only for the fatisfaction of her confcience, and by the orders of her father confeffors, who have refufed her abfolution ever fince fhe was married, becaufe of the ftate in which fhe lived with Monfieur de Gefvres.

III Whether at the time of her marriage with the faid Marquis de Gefvres, fhe was aged 17 years?

Said. yes

IV Whether, that the third and fourth night after their marriage they lay together, and that the marriage was confummated thofe two nights?

Says, it is true that the third and fourth night after their marriage, the faid Marquis de Gefvres lay with her, but that it is falfe that he either then or ever fince confummated the marriage.

V. Whether it be not true, that, though young, fhe was not ignorant what confummation of marriage was? And why, in feveral facts and articles upon which fhe caufed the faid Marquis de Gefvres to be interrogated, fhe affects to put on airs of an ignorance fo little probable?

Said, it is certain that at that time fhe did not know what confummation of marriage was

VI Whether the tendernefs fhe fhewed for the Marquis, on the Wednefday following, at his departure for the army, and which fhe teftified by her letters during the whole campaign, were the confequence and effect of the fatisfaction fhe had received from their conjugal union?

Said, it is true fhe at that time teftified by her letters a great deal of tendernefs for the faid Marquis de Gefvres, but that it was not the effect of the fatisfaction fhe had received from their conjugal union, but only becaufe fhe thought it was enough that he was her hufband, that they had been before the prieft, and received the benediction of the church.

VII. Whether, at his return from the army, about the beginning of November, he lay with her the very night of his arrival, continued to do so for two months and a half, and often performed the duties of marriage?

Said, it is true that the said Marquis de Gesvres, at his return from the army about the beginning of November, lay with her the very night of his arrival, and continued to do so all the time set down in the article and more, but that it is absolutely false to say that he performed the duties of marriage, whatever efforts he might make to do it

VIII. Whether, that at that time she thought herself with child, and said so to several of the family.

Said, that she never thought herself with child, never told any body that she was so.

IX. Whether, that at his return from the army about St. Martin's day, he lay with her at St. Owen, that as he was getting into bed, he smelt an ill smell in the bed, that the said lady told him it was some tenches which were put to her sides, and that notwithstanding the disagreeableness of the smell, he had the civility to stay with her, and to perform the act of marriage?

Said, it is true that he lay that night with her, the respondent, at St. Owen, but it is very false that he at that time performed the act of marriage

X. Whether she can so flatter herself as to think any body will believe her when she says, that, during all that time, she had been ignorant of the condition of husband and wife, and that in order to be acquainted with it, she had any need to go to the wedding of a lady of her acquaintance, who taught her a great many things which before she knew nothing of?

Said, that she thinks she may flatter herself so far, since it is true

XI. If it be not true, that the said Marquis being arrived at Gesvres, on All Saints day, staid there ten or twelve days, and that they lay together all that time like man and wife?

Said, it is true that the said Marquis de Gesvres lay

with her all the time set down in the article; but false that he either then or any time since, consummated the marriage, whatever attempts he might make to do it.

XII. Whether she will appeal to the persons who have seen the Marquis in a state of perfect erection?

Said, that the proposal is impertinent, and that she will appeal to none but the searchers.

XIII Whether she will believe the servants and landresses, who saw upon the cloths and in the shirts of the said Marquis de Gesvres, the tokens of the consummation of their marriage?

Said, no, and that the proposal is as ridiculous as the preceding, since he never did consummate the marriage, and for proof of what she says, she demands to have her person visited

It is to be observed, that these interrogatories were put into the hands of searchers, who were physicians, appointed for the purpose:—These they read over attentively to the parties before they proceeded to the visitation, or the inspection of the parts —The names of the four physicians were:

The Sieur Gayant, physician, and the Sieur Marechall, surgeon to the King, nominated on the part of the Marquis, and on the part of the lady, the Sieur Hequet, physician, and the Sieur Chevalier, surgeon.—The formula of both parties follow, and first that of the Marquis's searchers.

We have viewed, and carefully examined the Marquis de Gesvres, and find that his exterior parts serving for generation, have the requisite figure, size and dimensions; but as these conditions are not sufficient for judging of the consummation of marriage, because there is occasion for erection and ejaculation, which did not appear to us, we cannot absolutely decide, whether he be able to discharge the conjugal duties or not.

Paris.   (Signed)   *Gayant* and *Marechal.*

We have observed, that all the parts of the Marquis de Gesvres, are of a fitting consistence, figure, number, and largeness for performing the matrimonial duties: but because all these conditions are not sufficient for establishing virility, and his power to perform his duties, without the tokens of erection, which we saw nothing of, we are of opinion, that towards deciding whether he is capable of performing the matrimonial duties, there should appear in him some tokens of erection, and, because those very tokens of erection would not be of force enough to ascertain the consummation of marriage, we are of opinion, that it would be proper to visit the body of Madam de Mascranny, his spouse

(Signed) *P. Hequet* and *J. Chevalier.*

A third Report, including many other particulars, was produced shortly after

The Report made in pursuance of an Order of Court

We have, in a special manner, examined the exterior genital parts of the Marquis de Gesvres. we have observed, that he is advantageously provided with all his parts, having their natural consistence, colour, dimension, and figure   But, because erection accompanied with firmness and some duration, is also absolutely necessary towards proving the virile power, and we did not observe any such thing in him, during our inspection, we suspend our judgment touching his potency   We do not, however, infer, that there is impotency in him, from our not having seen that token of virility, because it does not always appear, and there are men to whom the presence of other men is an obstacle to the appearance of such a token   Therefore, we cannot decide concerning the potency of the Marquis de Gesvres, it being impossible to judge of such sort of things, without the tokens indicative thereof   It were to be wished, that the Marquis de Gesvres could have erection in our presence, at some other time. and in some other place more favourable to him, we might then decide concerning his condition.

Upon this acknowledged perfection of the parts, with respect to figure only, did the Marquis move for the non suitment of his wife, but against him it was expresly pleaded by the lady's advocate, that conformation alone, or the natural shape of the penis, is only a condition *sine qua non*, and that nothing was clearer than the position, " that figure and motion do not always meet in one and the same subject—There may be motion without figure, and figure without motion—what proves the latter beyond a doubt is, that the canon law has absolutely two different chapters, one entitled, *de Frigidis* of the cold, the other *de Maleficiatis*, of the ill-made Those men, like the Marquis, it is evident, are called the *frigid*, but the operations of the ill-made, were suppofed to be hindered by sorcery.

It is curious to obferve, that in cafes of impotency, in one of the parties, canons recommend chaftity to both! The canon we allude to, was made under Gregory I. but Gregory II. who fucceeded him, was too wife to fay any reftraint upon a woman's fuing for a divorce, he contented himself by fimply recommending the hufband of an ill-organized wife, to turn the conjugal life into a fraternal one Yet, perfuaded that every body has not the gift of continency, he concludes his difcourfe with thefe words *Sed quia hoc magnorum eft, fi non poteft fe continere, nubat* But, becaufe this is a great undertaking, if a perfon cannot contain himfelf he may marry again The fame thing that he allowed to the hufband of a difabled wife he granted to the wife of an impotent hufband, and the decrees of this pontiff are in general adhered to, at this prefent time.

But to return to the confideration of what it is that conftitutes the characters of frigidity and ill-make. it is to be noticed, that the firft is thus defined, in the canon we have referred to *frigidus is cenfetur qui licet habeat membrum, habet tamen inutile ad copulam, quia inerigibile quod melius facto poreft infpici buam verbis exprimi;* viz They are to be accounted frigid, who have the virile member perfect in form, but which is, notwithftand

ing, unuseful for copulation, because incapable of erection; which is a circumstance better understood by inspection than explained with words. Such a member,
saith the law, is good for nothing, because *oll. dura
quies nervos affereus urget somnus.* It is as it were dead,
and sleeps a sleep of iron, that is, it wants that motive
faculty which is the summit of its utility.—As visitations
for the purposes of inspecting virility, are not known in
this country, we shall be more particular in describing
them—" They manage these things better in France,"
for there, very little depends upon the oath of the accu-
sing party. The searchers, as we have before observed,
are men, and generally those somewhat advanced in years,
and in a business of this nature, they are instructed to lay
aside the language of judges, and talk to the parties as
cordial friends, officiously tending them their advice,
and more than this, like a favourable judge, who sometimes puts words in the mouth of a culprit at the bar,
they sometimes point out methods and expedients to the
impotent person, informing him how he may exhibit the
token of virility in its best appearance. They addressed
the Marquis de Gesvres in the following manner, when
they paid him the visit of inspection. " Sir, we readily
allow that the master of a law-office and four searchers,
are by no means the most inviting objects to put nature
in a good humour, and therefore, that not being the case
at this present instant, send for us any morning, and call
us into your chamber in the happy minute, when, within the privacy of four curtains, if that moment has not
arrived, you shall wait for that favourable glance from
nature's eye, which she never refuses long to persons of
your age, who are not entirely under her displeasure.—
Then happy shall we be to be witnesses of the alteration
she shall have wrought in you."

Thus indulgently they dealt with the Marquis, but,
after all their efforts, they could by no means give in
their ultimatum as favourable.—there is no doubt but
they made use of every incentive, for the French
lawyers inform us, that in many cases the searchers did

not merely truſt to the formation of the virile member in a ſtate of flacidity, but would often prick it, to diſcover whether it had feeling or not.   The duty of ſearchers is thus inculcated in one of the old law books. Debent inſpicere utrum homo moveatur ad libidinem, viz. they ought to ſee whether the man can be moved by luſt.

Before we proceed any further, in order to enter into the ſpirit of the pleaders on both ſides of this caſe, it will be neceſſary to ſhew the ſuperior accuracy and circumſtantiality of the French laws, by explaining ſome particular terms, ſuch as the Congreſs, the Viſitation, &c. the former of which is ſimpl nothing more than the act of copulation, in the preſence of an eccleſiaſtical judge app inted to ſee it done. this ceremony has been of late aboliſhed becauſe, in one caſe, it once led the judges into an error   And it has been ſince obſerved. that one happy or unhappy quarter of an hour, was ſufficient to fix a mans fate in a trial of this kind for ever, as it was exceedingly difficult, if a perſon generally impotent, could no find himſelf capable once in the courſe of a few months!—Viſitation or inſpection has been the ſubſtitute for the Congreſs, which being a real and local ſtate. is ever the ſame, and ſubject to no viciſſitude Again, the Congreſs depended upon the concurrence of two adverſe arties, one of whom, the wife, as the counſel obſerved might eaſily ſupplant the other, while the Viſitation requires no more of the wife than a little patience. which ſhe will gladly lend as a ranſom for her modeſty

Copulation is alſo defined to conſiſt of Motion, Penetration, and Expulſion, and conſequently as the evidence of the latter could only be obtained by the wifes perſon her evidence was always ſuppoſed to be ſufficient and therefore, as Madam de Maſeranny was ſuppoſed to ſay to her huſband, " The end of your marrying me was to make me paſs from my maiden condition to that of a wife, yet, after a long cohabitation, after many attempts and endeavours, you have left me the ſame as you found me, you are therefore culpable and inſufficient "

Visitation, and the testimony or oath of the wife, was further preferred, on account of the little dependance that could be made on the external appearance and conformation of the virile member in a man, and the canon law even illustrates the case of a lifeless member, in a simile from sacred writ, viz. for as the body without the spirit is dead, so also, &c &c. Still it is apparent, that the evidence of a wife is not always to be depended upon, supposing her to be actuated by malice, or regardless of an oath—The following case offers a shrewd suspicion of an instance of this kind—" A husband becomes a father, loses a wife, and proceeds to a second marriage. After several months cohabitation with his second wife, he goes a voyage to sea   During his absence this second wife marries another man, and the first husband, at his return home, is saluted with an accusation of impotency, which he answers by saying, I have had a child of my first marriage, but the wife insists upon it, that the birth of that child was only owing to his wife's having to do with another man   Behold the state of this contest, in which it is visible, that the searchers could not reasonably doubt of the faculties of one who had been a father!"

Still to proceed, there is a very great latitude in the notions, that the French lawyers, as well as the canon law, entertain of a temporary impotency in a man. Madam Mascranny's advocate insisted upon it, that the Marquis de Gesvres was afflicted with a palsy in the parts, and quotes Zachias, Tit 9 Book ix that author says he, tells us that a man's genitals sometimes fall into a palsy, that then there's an end of hope   all is lost! no resource left! And this not only when this evil seizes people who are upon the decline in point of years, but likewise when it attacks young folks: then says Zachias, nature loses the habitude of conveying the spirits towards the afflicted parts, and from thence it happens, that those spirits so entirely quit their channel, that they never reclaim it again.   And this is doubtless the reason why that grave author, the great Petrone, who has spoken so ill of the Canonists, puts these words into the mouth of a lady diffatisfied with her favourite, *paralifin cave*—Away, wretch! you are going into a palfy.

How juftly, fay the Canonifts, does all this apply to the text and rule of the apoftle · *Vir non habet poteftatem fui corporis fed mulier*—A man hath not power over his own body, but the woman.

But, notwithftanding a fuperb and pompous appearance of ability, is often fallacious; yet fuch perfons who can afford no fuch fhew, are juftly to be diftrufted, and as the French advocate goes fome length upon apparent capability, when the thing by no means exift, we fhall therefore make ufe of that part of his plea verbatim · " It is undeniably true, and is confirmed by the experience of all mankind, that the difference between able women's men, and thofe that are frigid, is this: In the former, the penis is contracted and fhrunk up, during the time that it does not actually ftand, fo that it is impoffible to judge of its length and thicknefs, unlefs it is erect and ftiff. Whereas it is quite the contrary in thofe that are frigid, as in the carcafe of a dead man. For fuch indeed have a penis, but it is never contracted or fhrunk up; it has a continual length and thicknefs, (as in other men when it ftands) but then it always hangs its head, and is incapable of a perfect and confiftent erection.—See Zachias upon this head in chapter concerning the tokens of virility and impotency.

It has been obferved, by all who have written concerning impotency, as well canonifts as phyficians, that there are many men whofe penis very readily rifes, nay, lifts itfelf up in a moft proud and oftentatious manner; but then it's fury is as foon fpent, like a fire made of ftraw, the moment it approaches its miftrefs's door, it bafely falls down at the very threfhold, and piteoufly vomits out its frothy foul (alluding to that verfe of Tibullus, Janua difficilis dominæ te verberet imber.) Thefe kinds of impotents are not rare nor unfrequent. Hoftienfis queries, whether they are to be ranked among the frigid, fince their vice proceeds not from the frigidity, but rather too much calidity of their blood. Of this fort of infirmity we have a noted inftance in the Baron du Pont, mentioned by Argentræus.

This Lord was feparated from his wife, Catharine de Parthenay, heirefs of Soubife, for impotency, Argentræus, in the article 429, of the cuftom of Bretagne, gives this defcription of his impotency : Quidam Juvenis valenti corpore uxorem inire non poterat, etii benè nafutus, fed fimul ac nervum admoverat, femen præcipitatâ feftinatione ejiciebat, ita ut nihil intrà injiceret, nec intromittere poffet genitale. He was a young man of a hale conftituon, but could not enter his wife's body, though rarely well hung ; for fo foon as he approached her with his penis, his femen flew off with fuch precipitation, that fhe was not at all the better for it, nor could his label of morality make its way into love's paradife.

Be that as it will, our infpectors warn us not to truft to the ftiffnefs of the virile organ ; there being in many an erective force, but not effective, becaufe not folid, fober, and ftrong enough to hold out to the end ; and therefore we muft always confult the wife's perfon, if we would know what has been done by the man, whether at firft fight he appears to be a man, or whether he does not. For though he appears to be a man, he is not prefently to be concluded fuch, becaufe there are fome whofe enfign of manhood is a mere cheat, gives mighty hopes, but performs nothing. Again, though he does not appear a man, it does not follow, that he is not a man ; becaufe the tokens of manhood do fometimes lie hid, and fometimes pop out. And therefore, by infpecting the hufband, no certain judgment can be made either for or againft virility ; but by infpecting the wife, both doubts are removed. For if in the wife, the feal of virginity appears to be broke, it is moft certain, both that the hufband has vigour, nay, and an efficacious vigour: but if the ſenſis remain whole and unhurt, there is, ſay the canons, a certain and violent ſuſpicion, that the vigour of the man, if it did exert itſelf, was fallacious; and if it did not exert itſelf, then there was the ſame ſuſpicion that nature had denied him it. And this ſuſpicion, though preſumptive, has the force of all undoubted proof, ſince the canons rely thereon, as appears per chapter Propoſuiſti, chapter Litteræ, and by all the doctors, to a man."

Having now produced the ſubſtance of every argument made uſe of upon this famous trial, on the part of the lady, we ſhall draw to a concluſion, without dwelling upon the arguments in favour of the Marquis, becauſe they are merely deſultory and ſophiſtical; and as ſuch they were treated; for, notwithſtanding all the influence of his family, and Madam Maintenon's interpoſition with the King on his behalf, nothing better could be obtained than an order from his Majeſty, that Madam de Maicranny ſhould continue to cohabit with the Marquis, till he was 25 years of age; as his father, the Duke, aſſured the King, that he himſelf was impotent till that period.—The Duke's family were not the moſt opulent in France, but the Lady had an eſtate of 4000l. per year, beſides a great ſum in ready caſh.

The ſecond octavo volume of this trial, which like the preſent, is ſwelled up by a number of caſes quite irrelative in any other eye than that of the law, contains examples of many artficial maidenheads——deſcriptions of ſmall orifices——ſuppoſed marks of virginity, impotency, &c.

The Trial of Mrs. Fanny Wilmot, wife of John Wilmot, Esq. M. P. for Adultery with Edward Washborn, a Footman. In 1790.

WILLIAM Garthwaite said, that he went to live as butler, in the family of John Wilmot, Esq. at his house in Bedford-Row, and continued to live in his service until some time on or about the 25th day of April last: and that John Wilmot and his wife Fanny Wilmot lived and cohabited together as lawful husband and wife, and had six children, viz. one son and five daughters, who are all now living, and the youngest of them about the age of five years; and that on all occasions, as far as he knew, they owned and acknowledged themselves to be lawful husband and wife, and for and as such they were and now are commonly accounted and taken to be, and that Mr. Wilmot, on all occasions, behaved to, and treated his wife with the greatest tenderness, love and affection.

He further said, that when he went to live with Mr. Wilmot, he kept nine domestic servants, viz. a butler, a coachman, a footman, an under footman, a lady's maid or own woman, an house-keeper, a nursery-maid, an house-maid, and a kitchen-maid, and that Edward Washborn lived there as footman, and continued there until February 1791. And this witness understood that Edward Washborn had lived in the family about seven years in all.

He further deposed, that unless his mistress Fanny Wilmot had female visitors, which was very seldom the case, she used every day to retire from table soon after she had dined, and go into the back drawing-room, where she mostly sat, leaving her husband with his children, in the dining-parlour. That about a fortnight after this witnefs went to live in the family, he began to remark, that Edward Wafhborn ufed to eat his dinner haftily, and go up ftairs to his miftrefs in the back drawing-room, under pretence to carry her dog victuals, and continued fuch practice until he left the family Upon thefe occafions he would ftay twenty, thirty, or forty minutes in the room with his miftrefs, until his mafter was about to leave the dining-parlour, which was known by his ringing the bell, for the butler to clear the tables ; when he has frequently feen Edward Wafhborn come down ftairs from his miftrefs, either with the coal-box in his hand, or the plate on which he had taken the dog's victuals. It was the cuftom he faid of his mafter and miftrefs to breakfaft in the dining-parlour; after breakfaft, his mafter ufed generally to go out and not return for fome hours, while his miftrefs ufed as conftantly after breakfaft to retire to the back drawing-room. It was the bufinefs of Edward Wafhborn, as footman, to clear away the breakfaft things, which after he has done, he has been frequently feen by this witnefs going into the back drawing-room to his miftrefs, where he has ftaid alone with her near twenty or thirty minutes , and this witnefs was the more particular in watching him, as he had fome fufpicions on his mind that there was too great a familiarity carrying on between him and his miftrefs.

And even after he was difcharged from the houfe and fervice of Mr. Wilmot, he ufed, notwithftanding, frequently, during the months of February, March, and April, to come and dine and drink tea with the fervants, as this deponent apprehends, chiefly by the invitation of Elizabeth Smith, the houfekeeper, by reafon that fhe would, upon thofe occafions, tell him fhe had afked Edward Wafhborn to come and dine with them, faying, it muft be very dull for him , but the latter remarked, it was generally in the abfence of Mr. Wilmot, or when he happened to dine abroad, that Wafhborn came ; and that at fuch times, Fanny Wilmot, foon after fhe retired from the dining-parlour, ufed to ring her drawing-room bell, which was in general anfwered by the footman, who, after going to his miftrefs, would return and tell Elizabeth Smith her miftrefs wanted her, who would thereupon go to her, but foon returning, he has obferved her to make private fignals to Wafhborn, fometimes by holding up one of her fingers, fometimes by pufhing him with her elbow, and fometimes by ufing particular geftures, and on receiving fuch private intimations, he ufed to leave the kitchen, or fervants' hall, and go up ftairs into the back drawing-room, and remain there alone with Fanny Wilmot, from twenty to forty minutes—This witnefs faid he could fpeak the more pofitively to the foregoing circumftances, on account of having ftrong fufpicions that an improper intercourfe fubfifted between her and Edward Wafhborn; he made it his bufinefs more particularly to have an eye upon their conduct.

Accordingly, he noticed, that one day laft April, his miftrefs had been for fome time looking from the front windows of the drawing-room into the ftreet, and on a fudden obferved, that fhe put on her hat and cloak, and went out into the ftreet, pulling the door after her; when, fufpecting the bufinefs, he foon afterwards went out into the ftreet himfelf, and on the oppofite fide of the way he faw Edward Wafhborn, but that he might not fuppofe this witnefs was upon the look-out, he afked him where Mr. Wilmot's fmith lived, and being informed, he immediately left him, pretending he was going to fuch fmith's, but ftill for fome little time kept his eye upon Wafhborn, whom he obferved to follow Mrs. Wilmot, but did not watch them further, being apprehenfive that they might obferve him fo doing.

On or about the 25th of March, he faid, that Elizabeth Barnes, Fanny Wilmot's own woman, having gone out, returned about eight o'clock in the evening, and foon afterwards came into the kitchen, and afked him if her miftrefs was from home, and upon his faying No, fhe faid, It was very odd, fhe had been trying to open the back drawing-room door, and found it faftened; he then took no notice to Elizabeth Barnes, but fufpecting that Edward Wafhborn might be locked up there with his

2

mistress, he communicated his suspicion to Samuel Clough, the footman, and desired him to go into the area where he could see every person who went out of or into the house, which Clough accordingly did; though previous to his speaking to Clough upon the subject, he went himself into the parlour in order to listen and be on the watch, and had remained there but a very short time before he heard the back drawing-room door open, and saw his mistress come down stairs, who seeing him, came into the dining-parlour and took up a newspaper, and looked at the same until he left the room and went down stairs into the kitchen. But while he remained on the listen on the kitchen stair-case, and almost immediately afterwards, he heard his mistress return up stairs, and presently come down again very softly, with another foot coming down stairs at the same time with her; both went along the passage, and he then heard the street door open very gently, upon which he crept up three or four stairs, and saw his mistress with the door in her hand about a quarter open, and gently shutting the same to, and she then returned, and having opened the back-door to let the dog in, went up stairs—He then went down stairs into the kitchen, and having joined Clough, he asked him whom he had seen go out at the street-door, who answered, Edward Washborn. From the foregoing circumstances he is firmly persuaded that Washborn had been locked up some time with his mistress, in the back drawing-room, that it was not known to any of the servants in the family, that Washborn was in the house, previous to Elizabeth Barnes returning home that evening as before-mentioned; so that he did verily believe, that he was let into the house on that occasion, privately, by Mrs. Wilmot, in the same manner as he was let out. This witness well remembered that his master was from home at the time, having an engagement to dine abroad on that day.

He further said, that on Sunday the tenth of April last, Mr. Wilmot dined abroad, and Mrs. Fanny Wilmot at home with Mrs Pascall, a lady of her acquaintance;

that just as the servants had finished their dinner, the drawing-room bell rung, which was answered by Samuel Clough, who, as he was going into the room, he saw Mrs. Pascall going out of doors with one of Mr. Wilmot's children, to take a walk, that Clough soon returned from the drawing-room, and on being asked what the bell rung for, he said, it was for Washborn (who had on that day dined with them in the kitchen) to go up to his mistress; and presently afterwards this witness saw Edward Washborn go up stairs, and heard his mistress speaking to him in the drawing-room, the door being open, in about five minutes afterwards, going up again softly, and observing the drawing-room door was shut, he then returned into the dining-parlour, determining to watch Washborn's coming down, and soon afterwards heard a creaking noise in the drawing-room, which he verily believes proceeded from his mistress and Edward Washborn's being upon the large sopha, which always stood in such room; and from such noise, which continued some minutes, he was induced to believe, that Fanny Wilmot and him were then and there committing adultery together; but after they had remained shut up in the drawing-room near thirty minutes, Washborn came down stairs and went into the kitchen, while, as he went up on a pretence to go into the back-drawing-room, he met his mistress on the landing-place, and observed she was without her hat, and that her hair appeared very much disordered, although at the time of dinner and afterwards, she wore a hat, and her hair appeared to be well dressed and powdered.

The pleasure of watching to discover what this witness pretended to know beforehand, must have been very great as having leave to go to the play one evening with some of the maid servants, he could not stay with them, but came home and got into the stable, where he sent for Samuel Clough, and desired him also to watch his mistress's motions!

William Tapscott, coachman to Mr. Wilmot, said, that living in the family ever since 1788, it appeared to him that his mistress frequently sought opportunities of being alone with her footman, Edward Washborn, and he was the more induced to notice her conduct by reason that, about a twelvemonth before that time, whilst the family were at the country-house at Wandsworth in Surry, he was passing by the breakfast-parlour window, and then observed that his mistress and Washborn were in the parlour, and that his arms was round his mistress's waist, which he immediately dropt on his passing by. And further, his mistress used in town, he said, (unless she had ladies to visit her, which was not often the case) to retire from table soon after she had dined, and go into her drawing-room, when Edward Washborn used to go as soon as he had dined, and carry her dog victuals in a plate and upon these occasions remain with her ten minutes, and sometimes a quarter of an hour together. He had several times noticed, as soon as his master's bell has rung for the butler to clear the dining-table, that Washborn has come running down stairs from his mistress, in order, as he apprehended, to avoid being seen with her by his master. And that after breakfast, as soon as his master was gone out, he used to go into the room to his mistress when she has been alone, where they have remained alone together for a quarter of an hour at a time.

Previous to the discharge of Washborn from the service of Mr. Wilmot, which took place in February last, he said he never knew his mistress to walk out unattended by some or one of the men-servants, but after that event he has observed her several times to walk out alone without any servant; and on the twentieth of April last, having heard from one of his fellow-servants that she was going to walk out, and suspecting she was going to Washborn's lodging, No 12, in Kings-street, Holborn, he was determined to watch her, and for that purpose went to a public-house fronting the street, where, about eleven o'clock in the forenoon, he saw her go into the house where Washborn then lodged; and in about three quarters of an hour afterwards he saw her come out, and Washborn following her to the door, and seeming as if he was speaking to her, and then bowing to her as she left him—He then saw her go into a child-bed ware-house next door, where she staid about six or seven minutes, and then came out again, and passed by the house from whence he had watched her, and she appeared as if she was walking home, but this witness, that he might not be observed by her, went a different way, and got home before her.

His master, he further said, on account of his being a Member of Parliament, and on account of his various other avocations was necessarily absent a great deal from his house in Bedford-row—But, between two and three o'clock in the afternoon of a day in April last, he well remembered it was on Easter Monday, he took a letter from his master to his fellow-witness, Mr Scatchard, at No. 12, in King-street, where Edward Washborn lodged, and while he was waiting in the passage for an answer, the parlour-door was opened by a servant, where he saw his mistress sitting therein, and folding up a letter, and when she had folded it, she rose, came out, passed the witness, and went up stairs; she then appeared in tears and greatly agitated, she enquired for a porter, and almost immediately afterwards this witness having received a letter from Mr Scatchard to his master, came away; and since that time, he said, that his master had not, to his knowledge or belief, cohabited with his wife.

Elizabeth Barnes, lady's maid in the family of Sir John Dalling, Bart in Upper Harley-street, said, that about June, 1786, she went to live in the family of John Wilmot, Esq in the capacity of own woman to Fanny Wilmot his wife; and continued to live in his family in that capacity, until the fifteenth of May last, and from the time she went to live in this family Mr. John Wilmot and Fanny his wife had six children, viz. one son and five daughters, all living——Five children, and all living! —What an age must this be, when matrons go a madding! There was nothing else material in this witness's evidence.

Ann Wisdom very *wisely* asserted, that in the evening of a day, a little before Christmas last, Edward Wash-

born, complaining that he was somewhat indisposed,
came up stairs and retired to his bed-room, the door of
which was opposite to the door of the nursery-room, divided by a narrow passage, in order, as she supposed, to
lay down : That about nine o clock the same evening,
the children being all in the drawing-room with her master and mistress, she left it, and came up stairs into the
nursery, and finding the deponent there, she sent her
down stairs to her own woman Elizabeth Barnes, who
was then in the kitchen, with a message, that she was to
go to the mantua-maker's, and desire her to come the
next morning to measure one of the young ladies for a
gown. She accordingly went down stairs, carried the
message, and returned immediately, and when she was
near the upper flight of stairs, she heard her mistress in
the passage between the nursery and Washbon's bed-room
and heard her go into the nursery where, when she went
in, she found her sitting, and did not then appear; or pretend to have any other business in the nursery, or for
waiting there, except the sending of her down stairs to
Elizabeth Barnes, for whom she might have rung the bell
in the drawing-room · and that from the circumstances
before deposed to, and her overhearing her in the passage
as beforementioned, and returning into the nursery, she
then suspected, and does now believe, that her mistress
took the opportunity of her absence to go into Washborn's
bed-room, where he then was.

Ann Frazer, spinster, house-maid, said, that about two
months after she went to live in the family, she began to
notice that her mistress took every opportunity of being
alone with Washborn, her footman, but the circumstance
that induced her to notice the same more particularly,
was her having one day about that time gone unexpectedly into the drawing-room, and found them alone together, when they both appeared much confused, her
mistress blushing exceedingly. From that time she said
she was cautious how she put herself in the way of breaking in upon them when she has known them to be alone
in a room together, as her mistress on the beforemention-

ed occasion seemed very angry, and remained so for several days, but she has frequently known them to be alone together in one of the drawing-rooms for twenty, thirty, and forty minutes at a time, and once in particular, some time in the month of January last, as she was cleaning the stove in the front drawing-room, Master Eardly Wilmot, her masters son, a child about eight years old, came up stairs from his dinner, and his mother, who was then in the back drawing-room, overhearing him, came to the door, and drove him down stairs again, chiding him very much for coming up to her without being sent for, this witness immediately suspecting that Washborn was with her mistress, went and listened, but happening to cough, she retired to her work, and immediately afterwards Washborn came out of the back drawing-room on tip-toe, and having peeped into the front drawing-room where the witness affected to appear quite engaged in her work, he immediately returned to his mistress in the back drawing-room, and remained with her until somebody knocked at the street-door, when he came out, and went down stairs nd answered it.

Jane Smith, spinster, kitchen-maid, affirmed, that in the forenoon of a day about three weeks after she went to live in the family, as she was going up stairs and passing the back drawing-room, the door being open, she saw her mistress and Edward Washborn standing by the fireside, and observed her mistress lay her hands familiarly and playfully on him, and turn him round

According to her evidence, after Washborn had left the family, he used to come into the house through the area, to see, as he said, Mrs. Smith, the housekeeper, and who used for the most part to keep him to dinner and tea; and after dinner this witness had several times observed her making signs to Washborn, upon which he would immediately go up stairs. And that at other times when Washborn has dined at the house, Mrs Smith has told him that her mistress wanted to speak to him about *a place !*—All the family, it seems, were very well acquainted with the situation of *the place* here alluded to.

Henry Hudfon, footman to Mr Bailey, in Bedford
Square, teftified to the fame circumftances as have been
before mentioned on the ground of undue intimacy between Wafhborn and his lady, adding, that after Wafhborn had taken lodgings at a houfe No 12, King-ftreet,
Holborn, he was twice fent to him by his miftrefs, once
with a parcel and a letter, and another time with a letter,
which he was to take to fome other perfon, and this witnefs faw him each time at thefe lodgings : and on Eafter
Monday laft in the evening, by his mafter's order, he took
a letter to his miftrefs at Wafhborn's lodgings, together
with her favourite dog, and as from that time his miftrefs
never returned home again, during his ftay in the family, it may be faid, fhe was turned out, as an old adage
expreffes it, *Dog and all !*

Perrot Fenton, of Doctors Commons, London, Gentleman, being fworn, faid, that on Friday the 15th of A-
pril laft, he was fent for to the Chambers of Meffrs.
Wilmot, Dunn, and Lancafter, Solicitors in Lincoln's
Inn, and on going thither was introduced to John Wilmot Efq and confulted as to the meafures neceffary to be
taken on his part, in confequence of his having then re-
cently been informed that his wife carried on a criminal
correfpondence with Edward Wafhborn, a difcarded
footman, who then lodged at a houfe, No 12, in King-
ftreet, Holborn, and when this witnefs had confidered
the circumftances of the cafe, he confulted counfel thereon, and by the advice of counfel he went to the houfe in
King-ftreet, on Saturday the fixteenth of the fame month,
and engaged apartments as for an acquaintance, of the
name of Marfhall, that fuch apartments confifted of a
dining or front room on the firft floor, and a back-room
on the fecond floor of the houfe, but Mr. Marfhall, whom
he then intended to place in fuch lodging, difappointing
him, he applied to his fellow-witnefs Mr Scatchard, and
prevailed on him to occupy them for the purpofe of dif-
covering whether Mrs. Wilmot really did or did not carry on a criminal correfpondence with Wafhborn. Accordingly, Mr. Scatchard took poffeffion on Monday

the 18th of April, and occupied them till Monday the 25th, when, to avoid suspicion, this witness was constrained to introduce Mr. Scatchard to the house by the name of Marshall, where this witness very frequently visited him, and several times had opportunities of viewing the room then occupied by Washborn, and other parts of the house, though it was not till the 20th of April that he had an opportunity of being certain that Mrs Wilmot and Washborn were locked up together, and alone in the chamber of the latter, when he had no doubt of their commission of the crime of adultery together.

But on Saturday the 23d of April, this witness again called on Mr. Scatchard, in King street, who informed him that the lady was just come to the house, and was then in the next room with Washborn, and presently after Thomas Scatchard had communicated such information, this witness left the house, and went to Mr. Wilmot, who was then waiting in the neighbourhood, and consulted him as to the adviseableness of breaking into the room wherein Fanny Wilmot and Edward Washborn were shut up, and afterwards quitting Mr. Wilmot, and returning to No. 12, King-street, he saw his fellow-witness, Mr. Scatchard, standing on the ballustrade of the staircase, and looking through the lights or little windows into the bed-chamber, when Mr. Scatchard informed him, that Washborn and the lady were in the nook or corner, between the bed and the fire-place, and that the bed-curtains not being drawn forward, he had been able to observe the motions of the parties, that the lady had been crying, and that Edward Washborn had been soothing and caressing her. This man then took the place of his fellow-witness, and observed that the shutters of the first and third sashed windows of the bed room were closed, and that the parties were retired into the nook or corner near the fire-place—their persons could not be seen from the situation he was then in, but on turning to the looking-glass which hung against the pier, between the second and third sashed windows, he saw, by the reflection, the heads of Fanny Wilmot and Edward Washborn, and was convinced they were then fitting clofe together on the left fide of the bed, and were kifling together. Prefently afterwards Wafhborn appeared to fink or kneel before the lady, while the reflection of her head only remained vifible to the witnefs on the looking-glafs, by reafon that the fame was fo hung, as not to reflect the lower part of the bodies of the parties, though he obferved the tefter of the bed and the curtains to be agitated or fhaken, and particularly obferved the head of Fanny Wilmot in motion, and upon the whole, from all the circumftances then under his obfervation, he did at the time believe that fhe then fat on the fide of the bed, and that Wafhborn knelt before her, and that in that pofition they committed adultery together. And he alfo faid, that after he had for fome time viewed the premifes, he gave place to his fellow-witnefs, Thomas Scatchard, who took another view, and then expreffed the like opinion to him. and further, that after Fanny Wilmot and Edward Wafhborn had remained together about an hour, or an hour and a half, according to the beft of his recollection, Mr. Scatchard went out of the houfe into the ftreet, to watch Fanny Wilmot on her return from thence, and this witnefs remained there, and by means of the lights in the partition, he foon afterwards faw Fanny Wilmot and Edward Wafhborn ftanding together, near the middle of the chamber, with their hands joined, they were in very earneft difcourfe, and appeared to be greatly agitated, and frequently lifted their joined hands up towards Heaven, and feemed to the witnefs to be plighting vows to each other, and that after they for fome time had remained thus, they paffed towards the door of the chamber, while he retired up ftairs to the landing-place on the fecond-floor, and then heard one of them undo the faftenings on the infide of the chamber-door, and come out, when Fanny Wilmot faid fomething in a low tone of voice, which appeared to him to be a fuggeftion that there was fome perfon watching them, as Edward Wafhborn came forward, and ftepped up two or three of the fecond flight of ftairs, and then returned,

saying, " Oh no, there is not !" This witness then looking over the balluftrades of the ftair-cafe, which is a well
ftair-cafe, faw Wafhborn going down ftairs, and Fanny
Wilmot following him, and prefently heard the ftreet-
door fhut to, and then faw Edward Wafhborn pafs up
ftairs, and go into his chambei, and open the fhutters of
the firft fafhed window

But the difcovery on the part of Mr. Wilmot himfelf,
it feems. did not take place till the 26th of April, when,
as this witnefs was at breakfaft with Mr. Scatchard, with
the dining room door a little opened, they heard a rapping at the ftreet-door, and thereupon heard Wafhborn
open his chamber-door, run down ftairs, and return up
ftairs, converfing with a woman, who accompanied him
into his chamber, when one of the parties faftened the
door of the chamber on the infide—And it having been
previoufly determined, between Mr. Wilmot and this
witnefs, that the correfpondence between Mrs Wilmot
and Wafhborn fhould be expofed that morning, this witnefs then went to Mr. Wilmot, at a houfe in the neighbourhood, leaving his fellow witnefs to make fuch dif-
coveries as he was able. About half an hour afterwards
he returned to King-ftreet, with Mr. Wilmot, whom he
introduced to the gentlewoman of the houfe, in a parlour
on the ground-floor, and, after ftaying fome time be-
low ftairs, and endeavouring to calm the agitation of
Mr. Wilmot, and do away the furprize and apprehenfion
of the people of the houfe, he went up ftairs, and on the
firft flight he obferved Mr Scatchard looking through
certain holes which he had made in the wainfcot, which,
as he afterwards found, commanded a view of the nook,
or corner, between the bed and fire-place beforementioned, he then paffed Mr Scatchard, and went on the
fecond flight of ftairs, and looked into the chamber, and
obferved that the fhutters of the firft and third fafh windows were clofed, and that Fanny Wilmot and Edward
Wafhborn were ftanding together between the bed and
the fire-place, he foon afterwards heard the bar let down
on the infide of the door of the chamber, and the lock

turned, and faw the door opened, and Edward Wafhborn come out, warily drawing the door to after him——this
witnefs then advanced to him, and gave him a letter addreffed to Mrs. Wilmot, and ordered him to deliver it
to Mrs Wilmot, whereupon he appeared furprifed and
confounded, but on his faying he knew Mrs. Wilmot was
in the room, Wafhborn withdrew with the letter, and
again faftened the door on the infide.   This letter was
written by Mr. Wilmot, informing her of his having difcovered her infidelity, and infifting that fhe fhould not
return to his houfe, recommending it to her to advife
with her friends, promifing to fend her linen, and wear-
ing apparel, and to furnifh her with money occafionally.
When this letter was delivered, Mr Wilmot went up
ftairs to the dining-room, and tenderly expreffed great
apprehenfion for the perfonal fafety of Mrs Wilmot;
left the fhame of the difcovery fhould be too much for
her——But foon afterwards Mrs. Wilmot came out of the
chamber, and was accofted by her hufband, who led her
into the oppofite dining-room, where fuch a fcene en-
fued between them as made this witnefs very apprehenfive that Mr. Wilmot would be overpowered by the
poignancy of his feelings, efpecially as he knew he was
not in a good ftate of health——While Mr. Wilmot and
Fanny Wilmot were converfing together, this deponent
and his fellow witnefs, went into the chamber, and obferved that the bed was greatly tumbled——At length Mr.
Wilmot and this witnefs withdrew from the houfe, but
Mrs. Wilmot ftaid there ; in the afternoon of the fame
day, this deponent again faw and converfed with her,
and about nine o'clock in the evening of the fame day he
again faw and talked with her, in Wafhborn's chamber,
Wafhborn being prefent. and Fanny Wilmot then informed the witnefs that fhe intended to fleep that night in
the houfe, and he was afterwards informed, and believes,
fhe did remain at the houfe until the next morning   He
further faid, he was well affured that Mr. John Wilmot
is a Member of Parliament, a Mafter in Chancery, and
a Commiffioner of American Claims, and that his vaū-

ous avocations muft neceffarily have occafioned him to be abfent a great deal from his houfe in Bedford-row.

It further appeared, that about noon on the aforefaid Monday, Mr John Wilmot caufed the trunks and boxes in Wafhborn's apartments in King-ftreet to be fearched by a peace-officer, in the prefence of him John Wilmot, Fanny Wilmot his wife, Edward Wafhborn, this deponent, and his fellow-witnefs, Thomas Scatchard, and that in the trunks, or boxes, there were found a parcel of guineas wrapped up in paper, and a large affortment of fafhionable and new cloaths, but no letters, and, on being queftioned by this witnefs, Wafhborn in the prefence and hearing of his miftrefs, acknowledged that he had received many letters from her, and that he had burnt them on the preceding day, which Mrs. Fanny Wilmot, on being queftioned by her hufband, acknowledged fhe had written and fent letters to Edward Wafhborn——There were alfo divers prints and drawings which Mrs. Wilmot and Edward Wafhborn then acknowledged had belonged to her, and that fhe had given the fame to him, and alfo a fhirt-pin, fet with hair, wrapped in filver paper, and appeared to be quite new, an elegant fancy gold ring, fet with hair, a box with curious fhells, a nutmeg grater in the fhape of a heart, a pocket-book, an ink-ftand. two riding-whips, a ftraw-box, and a bottle of fweet water with a label bearing the infcription of "Eau de Cologne," and various other articles. And as for the hair in the head of the fhirt-pin, Mrs. Wilmot acknowledged it was her own.

It further appeared, that while Mr. Wilmot was in great diftrefs of mind, on account of his wife's infidelity, and the neceffity there was for preferving appearances, till he could obtain fufficient evidence of her guilt, he informed the refpondent of his having been applied to give a character of Wafhborn to Colonel Popham, and feveral times expreffed the embarraffment he laboured under on that account, but this witnefs advifed him to give fuch a character, he did fo, and it was fince believed that Wafhborn was, by appointment, to go, and did go, to his place at the faid Colonel Popham's, late in the evening of the twenty-fifth of April laft.

This witnefs, in refpect to what he faw in Wafhborn's room, faid, that on Saturday the twenty-third day of April, he obferved the reflection of the heads of Fanny Wilmot and Edward Wafhborn, face to face, and afterwards faw the reflection of her head in motion, and alfo a tremulous motion in the tefter and curtains of the bed, and after that Fanny Wilmot and Edward Wafhborn ftanding hand in hand together, and converfing together in an earneft and agitated manner.

He further faid, that he furnifhed his fellow-witnefs, Thomas Scatchard, with gimblets of all the fizes he could meet with in an ironmonger's, with fome or one of which he made three or four holes in different parts of the wainfcot of the room, by means of which they found the whole of the nook or corner to which the parties ufed to retire, might be fully view'd, but, from an apprehenfion of being called on as a witnefs, and believing Thomas Scatchard would be fully competent to the proving the adultery between the parties, he modeftly felt himfelf averfe to looking through the hole, while he fuppofed the parties were committing adultery together, but, at length, on being ftrongly urged by his fellow-witnefs, he did for a moment look through one of the holes, juft before Edward Wafhborn opened the door, but Fanny Wilmot was then ftanding fo clofe to the wainfcot, that he could not fee any thing but her gown, by that means he efcaped being put to the blufh!

Neither could he fay he ever faw the miniftrant and Wafhborn lying down together on the bed in the room; nor take upon himfelf to depofe pofitively to an act of adultery between them, but he was witnefs to fo many approximate acts, that he has not any doubts in his mind, but that they did frequently commit adultery together.

It is now worth while to obferve Mrs. Wilmot's confidence in denying the charge of adultery, as the time when fhe was leaving Wafhborn's chamber, in order to return home, this witnefs ftepped up to her and introduced

her to her hufband, who was at his elbow; at which
Mrs. Wilmot appeared as though fhe affected to be furr-
prifed at the producent's charging her with adultery, and
repeatedly affured him he was miftaken, and even folemn-
ly declared fhe was entirely innocent of that crime, ear-
neftly foliciting that her oath might be taken, as to her
being innocent of the fame. Wafhborn alfo forced himfelf into the company, and made the like declarations,
and offered to take his oath to the fame purport, and
they both contended that the producent ought to be fatisfied with fuch their oaths, and this witnefs had no doubt
but that they would have taken their oaths accordingly;
but he confidered this part of their conduct to be part of
a plan concerted between them, and further confidered
Wafhborn's intrufion fo improper, that he repeatedly
drove him from the prefence of the producent. Mrs.
Wilmot at firft, he faid, urged there was nothing improper in her conduct, and even after the circumftances
which could be adduced in evidence againft her, were
ftated, fhe defired fhe might be allowed to clear herfelf
on oath, and then that her little indifcretions might be
forgiven! and fhe particularly defired Mr Wilmot
would not mention the matter to his father and family.
And, lawyer-like, after obtaining an account of the feveral charges which were to be made againft her, fhe afked
whether the refpondent and his fellow-witnefs, Thomas
Scatchard, would take upon themfelves to fwear, that they
had feen *an abfolute act* of adultery, and on being anfwered in the negative, fhe addreffed herfelf to the refpondent, and faid, as fhe obferved that the producent acted
under his opinion, fhe defired to argue the cafe with him
and then contended, as the producent could not prove a
pofitive act of adultery, he could not avail himfelf of the
circumftances of the cafe, fo as to obtain a divorce!!!

A Deputy's lady in the city hearing this part of the
trial, exclaimed, to *largeft half*, "Dear dear, Mr Dum-
pling, did you ever hear fo much *impertence* in all your
born-days!"

All the witnesses proved that the house of Mrs. Page, where Washborn lodged, was a decent house, as well as that Mrs Page was a very discreet woman!

Thomas Scatchard, of Wardrobe Place, Doctor's Commons, London, went exactly over the same ground as the last witness, but was very particular in asserting that he plainly saw the curtain shake, that having looked for some time, he gave place to his fellow-witness, Perrot Fenton, who also looked for some time, and then gave place to him again, who, on looking again, by the help of the looking-glass which hung against the pier between the second and third windows, observed, that Washborn, and Mrs. Wilmot had come more forward into the room and saw them embrace and kiss each other several times, till Washborn sunk down before such lady, out of his sight —But, previous to this, by opening the holes in the wainscot, he very plainly saw Washborn and Mrs Wilmot standing together between the bed and fire place, and apparently in conversation, that presently afterwards they sat down on the bed-side close to each other, when Edward Washborn took the lady by the left hand and kissed the same, and when he had so done, he stooped a little, and with his right hand pulled up her petticoats a-above her knees, so that this witness could plainly see her naked thighs, that he then stooped and kissed her naked thigh once or twice, and having so done, this witness saw him put his right-hand up her petticoats, which she seemed rather to resist, but they soon got up, and stood face to face, when he observed that the flap of Washborn's breeches was unbuttoned, that Edward Washborn again put one of his hands up the petticoats of such lady, and his other hand round her waist, she making some little resistance, and standing cross-legged, and that having stood for some time in this situation, the lady appeared to be moving as if she were about to go away.

Mary Page, of King-street, Bloomsbury, widow, said, that some time in the beginning of Febuary 1791, Edward Washborn applied to her to take an apartment or lodging in her house, and conceiving him to be a gentle man, and having received a character of him as such, she immediately agreed to let him have the use of a bed-room in her house, where he lived for eleven weeks, during which, he was several times visited there by Mrs. Elizabeth Smith, Mr Wilmot's house-keeper, whom this witness and her servant then understood, and believed to be, his aunt

She added, that in about a fortnight after, he began to be visited by a female person, about twice in the course of every week, during the time he resided there. This female was always let into and out of the house by Edward Washborn, and they were always together in his bed-room, and alone, but she did not think they ever remained together at such visits for a considerable time

Richard Townsend, and John Serjeant, of Doctor's Commons, London, Gentlemen, proved the marriage of the parties

This very singular cause was first brought into the Consistory Court of London—and from thence an Apeal was made to the Arches Court of Canterbury, where a Sentence of Divorce was obtained.

————

This trial, it should be remarked, is destitute of a circumstance which has certainly distinguished a great number of the kind—which is, that the lady's confidante has not become the principal witness against her!

The Trial of George Davidson, at Newcastle upon Tyne, in August, 1774; for a Rape upon Isabella Blair.

THE following trial, as well as some others which appears in the course of this Work, occurring at an assize in the country, never appeared before in any collection whatever, and but for the assiduity of the Editors might have entirely escaped the cognizance of our readers.

Doctor Scott said, that about the 21st of January last, Isabella Blair applied to him at Stannerton, where he practises physic: that she told him how she had been used by the prisoner, and was advised to come to him for his advice. The doctor said that he did not examine her closely; she complained of a pain and weakness in her back, and a pain in one of her legs and knee, which he found were inflamed and swelled. She told him that she had been four days in coming from the place where she lived to him, which is about ten miles—he gave her some medicines, and called afterwards to see her, and told her that the distance was too far for him to attend her properly, and to administer the quantity of medicines her disorder required; and, likewise, that it would be necessary for her to apply to the Infirmary at Newcastle, where she would have the care taken of her that the distemper required, and get the assistance of the faculty of that house. He was then asked by the court, if he thought the usage she met with from the prisoner was the occasion of that disorder she complained of? he said, that in the manner she told him the circumstances, he made not the least doubt but it was. That, as

far as he had examined, complaints of that nature
might come by cold

Doctor Rotheram said, that Isabella Blair came
as a patient to the infirmary about the middle of
February last; he being attending physician that
week, she was under his care   That she told him
the circumstances in the same manner as she had
spoken in court   He then examined her very mi-
nutely, and found the vagina very much depressed
and inflamed.   That these circumstances appeared to
him as if she had been lain with by a man.   On the
doctor being asked with regard to her knee and leg
he agreed with what Mr   Scott had said.   He said
he would not have the jury understand him that
the inflammation and swelling might not be occasioned by cold, as it was a rheumatic complaint —
On his being asked if the prosecutrix's recovery
was any ways doubtful? he said he looked upon her
to be in a very dangerous way, as the disorder had
fallen on her lungs —He was further asked, if a woman who had never known man, might not appear,
on examination, as if she had.   He said it was very
obvious that a woman might be deflowered by a
fall, &c. though she had never known man.

Isabella Blair said, that she lived with Mr. Potts,
at Mason Dinnington Hill-head, on the 12th of November, 1773, on which day she had leave to go to
Stannerton to see her mistress's grand-children
dance, who resided there ; that on her return home
she called in at a public-house at Mason Dinnington,
with desire to go see the dancers, as there was a
dancing-school in that town, where she met with
the prisoner at the bar, George Davidson, drinking,
who was hired to her mistress, he desired her to
sit down, on which she told him he had more need
to go home to his wife than to be sitting there spen-
ding his money.   The prisoner then told her that
his wife had taken the child that day along with
her to go and see her (the prisoner's wife's) mother.

She then replied, he ought to be the more careful during her absence, and defired of him, as it was late, to fee her home. The prifoner then told her, if fhe would ftop a little he would go with her. He then called for fome more liquor, and fhe went to fee the dancers, and on her return fhe found the prifoner ftill drinking; fhe again folicited him to go home with her, he then told her he would have a-nother pot, and then he would go with her. On this fhe became very uneafy, and told him fhe muft be going; he then faid, as foon as the liquor was out he would go with her, and at the fame time added, he would lye with her in the way home. She then replied, "No, George, I hope not—I dare t uft myfelf with you, as I think you are a better man than to do any thing to harm me." Upon this they came away together, and he was very peaceable till they were better than half way (this diftance was better than a quarter of a mile) and then he took hold of her and threw her down on the ground —She, amazed at this treatment, afked him what he meant to do: he anfwered, he would lye with her; fhe faid, For God's fake, George, rather take my life, for the one will be as agreeable as the other : he was then preparing to lye with her.

Court. What do you mean by preparing to lye with you ?—He was letting down his breeches.

She then turned herfelf on her face ; the prifon-er then pulled up her cloaths behind ; fhe then ftrug-gled with him and got upon her feet; upon this, he caught hold of her by the ancle, and fhe fell upon *her knees : he now took hold of her by the* left arm, and twined her over on her back ; fhe fhout-ing with all her might, he put his hand upon her mouth ; whilft fhe ftruggled as much as fhe was a-ble, till, quite fpent, fhe could make no more refift-ance. He then took hold of her by the legs and dragged her over five or fix ridges of the field.

At this part of her examination the profecrutrix

fainted, and coming to herself again, was informed by the court not to think any shame, as there was a necessity of her explaining every circumstance.

The prisoner then laid himself upon her, and had carnal knowledge of her body.

Here she fainted a second time—On her recovery—

Court Did the prisoner enter your body?—Yes.

Court. Did you feel any thing come from him?—Yes.

She fainted a third time

On being asked if the prisoner left her after this usage, and if she went home immediately, she said, she had not power to move from the ground, that he sat upon the dike opposite to her for about a minute, and then he came and used her in the same manner as he had done before. He then raised her from the ground, and bid her go home; she not being able to stand, sunk down on her knees. The prisoner then d——d her for a b——h, and asked her if she had got drunk. That she then desired the prisoner to go and get somebody to take her home, that the prisoner then left her for some time, and returned again, saying he had been to get her brother, but that he could get none of the family to hear, for they were all in bed. He then used her in the same manner as before, she not being able to make any more resistance. And after that he thrust something hard up her body, which to her seemed as if he was tearing out her bowels, that she supposed it must have been his hand, and he likewise put an old tobacco-chew there, which she took out of that place herself; that from the anguish and pain, she was in a state of insensibility, and could remember no more

William Blair said, that the night on which it happened, which was on the 12th day of November last, Isabella Blair, his sister, went to Starneror hopping. That about half past ten o'clock tha night, as he was standing in the house where he lived, he heard something like a rap at the door, when, on his opeuing it, his fiter fell into his arms. That is soon as he brought her in and saw her in the light, her cap was off, as was likewile her handkerchief, her breaft was bare, and her cloaths torn and dirty. He afked her what was the matter. She told him fhe had been very badly ufed in fuch a field, and that fhe had in ftruggling loft her bundle, and upon her deferibing the place, he immediately took a lanthorn and candle, and went to the place in the field where it had happened ; when he came there he found the grafs laid down for about five ridges, as if fomebody had been lying and tumbling there. that he found his fifter's cap, handkerchief, &c. filver button ; the cap and handkerchief were torn, (they were produced in court) that he then brought them home, where he found his fifter in a very weak condition. fitting in an arm-chair : on his being afked if he was then informed of her fituation, and the perfon who had uled her fo, fhe faid, George Davidfon.

Roger Mafon, faid, that the night on which this affair happened he was at work in the byar ; that his work being done, he came into the room where Ifabella Blair was ; he found her fitting in an armchair by the fire—her brother was ftanding with his back towards her—that fhe feemed to this deponent to be very ill—that her breaft and head were bare, and her hair hanging about her fhoulders —her brother got a lanthorn and candle and defired him to go along with him in fearch of her cloaths —that he went with him to the field, where they found the grafs. fome trodden down, and her cloaths were found in that place—On his being afked if he faw the prifoner that night, he faid he did not fee him till the next day, when he (the prifoner) afked after Bella. this deponent then told him he had *behaved* to her in a very bafe manner, and which he was afraid he would have reason to repent of. The prisoner then told him he was very much in liquor, and that if he had behaved ill to her he was very sorry for it.

Mrs. Potts said, that Isabella Blair was servant to her at the time the affair happened. That on the 12th of November last, she sent her to Stannerton hopping, and to see her grand-daughter dance, as there was a dancing-school at Mason Dinnington that on her return home she was in a very miserable condition, her cloaths being very dirty, her cap and handkerchief off, her hair hanging on her shoulders; that she asked her if she had met with any person who had used her badly? she answered, she had; and by one whom they all knew, and that it was their George, who had used her in a very barbarous manner. On being asked what he had done to her, she said he had lain with her against her will. On the deponent's being asked if she had examined her body or her linen? she said her linen she did, but not her body, and found the back part of her shift very wet, which she supposed was with the prisoner's dragging her over the grass—and on being asked if there was any blood appeared upon it? she said, No; but that there was blood on her arm—and on her being further asked in regard to her health before this happened, she said that she had lived with her two years and a half, and that she never knew her ill in that time, but once of an ague, of which she got the better, and had her health afterwards as well as she had before, till this misfortune happened—And on being asked if ever the prosecutrix was given to keep company with the men, or behaved herself any ways indecent, she said she never saw any thing of the kind by her, but thought her much the reverse; and that a better servant could not be about any person's house than she was.

Court. Now, prisoner, if you have any thing to say in your defence, now is your time?—No.

Court. Have you any person to call to your character?—Call John Pringle and Ann Rutter.

John Pringle refused being sworn; said he knew little of the prisoner, and would choose to have nothing to do in it, as he could do him no good.

Ann Rutter sworn. Said she kept a public-house at Mason Dinnington; that the prisoner had been several times in her house, that she thought him an honest man, and never saw any thing ill by him. On her being asked if ever she saw Isabella Blair with the prisoner in her house? she said, that on the 12th of November last, in the evening, she did. Being asked if she heard or saw any indecencies pass between them? she said, no further than when Isabella Blair asked him to see her home, he told her if he did he would kiss her by the way. Being asked in what manner the prisoner expressed himself, and whether she thought it was in jest or in earnest? she said, she thought it was spoken in jest. She was further asked, whether she thought the prisoner in liquor or not? she said, she thought he was not, as he could speak and walk very well.

The Judge then summing up the evidence to the Jury in a very clear and impartial manner—they, without going out of court, found him Guilty.

Judge Blackstone then passed sentence of Death upon the prisoner.

There are two leading features in this trial, which in many cases, would have terminated in mercy to the prisoner; that is to say, his being solicited by the prosecutrix to go home with her, though in a state of intoxication, and notwithstanding he had in some degree made his conditions for so doing, by forewarning her that he should kiss her or lye with her, if he did. There can be no doubt, but that in a circumstance of this kind, with respect to the term *kissing*, it may be said with much propriety, that more was meant than meets the ear! for if this threat, or rather bargain, had been meant simply of a salute with the lips, there would have been little hazard in the prisoner's venturing of that, even in the public-house, especially in the season of dancing and festivity. However, the state of intoxication, and what followed as the consequences of it, though tinctured with wantonness and barbarity, was dearly atoned for, in the sacrifice of a life that might probably have repaired the injury sustained.

The Trial of Mrs. Timmings, for Adultery, in the Consistory Court of London; March 20, 1791.

THE marriage being proved, Thomas Gillet, nephew and apprentice to Mr. John Timmings, in Steward-street, near Bishopsgate-street, said, that after he became journeyman and foreman to Mr. Timmings, he very well knew Mr. J. Smith of Aldgate, and that Mr. and Mrs. Timmings always lived together as man and wife, till the month of January or February last, when Mrs Timmings's unlawful connection with Mr. Smith and others, was first discovered. Mr. Smith, he said, he knew particularly, by his bringing shoes to the house, and coming backwards and forwards as an acquaintance of his master and mistress. On the 12th of February, he said, that on Mr. Timmings's going out, he told him, the witness, that he was going to Greenwich; and that between eight and nine o'clock on the same evening, Mr Smith came to the house; and he soon afterwards saw him in the kitchen, in company with Mrs. Timmings and Mary Gibbs, a maid-servant. From communications made to the witness by this maid servant, with respect to the conduct of Mr Smith and his mistress, prior to this period, he said, he suspected a criminal connection; and had, therefore, made a cavity through the wainscot of the kitchen, on purpose to make use of the first opportunity to observe their behaviour. As this kitchen was on the ground-floor, he found the stair-case a very convenient place; and accordingly, soon after Mr. Smith came in, having placed himself there, he kept his situation near two hours, during which time he saw the maid dress a fowl, upon which herself, Mr. Smith, and her mistress supped. Soon after this, Mary Gibbs put on her hat and cloak and went out, and left them together; this was near eleven at night but as the witness still kept his position, he soon observed Mr Smith draw his chair towards Mrs. Timmings, and put his left hand round her neck, while she laid her head on his shoulder. He then kissed her, and put his right-hand up her petticoats towards her private parts, in which situation, after they had remained some time, the witness observed her petticoats drawn up, though he did not exactly see by what means; however, he was certain that Mr Smith was then upon her, between her legs, though he could not see whether his breeches were down or not, however, he plainly observed his body in motion, while laying upon his mistress, in a chair; from all which circumstances, he had no manner of doubt but they were then in the act of copulation, and had the carnal use and knowledge of each other's bodies. But while they were in this situation, he observed Mr. Timmings rush into the kitchen, from a door leading to the yard, and addressing himself to Mr. Smith, said, "You rascal, how dare you come to my house and use my wife in this manner!" on which the deponent left his situation and went into the yard, and from thence into the street, when he heard Timmings say, "Out, out, out, with you," and heard the street-door shut, and Mrs. Timmings say, "Forgive me, for-

give me, I'll do fo no more!" he left his aforefaid fituation at the time by him predepofed to; he did not fee
whether the faid James Smith's breeches were down or
not as articulate   He added, that he did not of his own
knowledge know, that Mr. Timmings was apprized of
the fituation of the faid perfons, and did not fee him from
the time of his leaving his houfe to go to Greenwich, until he faw him rufh into the kitchen.   That, foon after
Mr. Timmings came into the ftreet, where he and the deponent met, he appeared very much agitated, infomuch
that he begged the deponent to fupport him, and they
went to the houfe of Grace Timmings, his mother, in
Bifhopfgate-ftreet, where he ftaid about a quarter of an
hour, and then with his aunt, Amey Barket, returned to
his houfe, he went there the next day, and faw Mrs.
Timmings go from thence, fince which he never faw
her there, but had conftantly feen her hufband reliding
there.

Mrs. Grace Timmings, widow, of Bifhopfgate ftreet,
faid, that Mr. Chamberlain, of White Lion-ftreet, Cha-
pel Yard, being indirectly charged by her fon with being connected with his wife, he agreed to come and fet-
tle the matter with the latter at his houfe in Union-ftreet
—he came accordingly, and Mr Timmings, Mr. Chamberlain, Mrs. Timmings, and herfelf, all went together
into the fore parlour, Mrs Timmings's father, Mr. Peter Huet, of Hackney, was alfo prefent—Mr. Timmings
then afked her, in the prefence of them all, whether fhe
did not go with Mr Chamberlain to an houfe of ill-fame
in Winchefter-ftreet, on the preceeding Thurfday? to
which fhe anfwered, Yes——He then afked her what paffed there? to which fhe anfwered, that Mr. Chamberlain
took her up into a back room, and committed adultery
with her—Mr. Timmings then afked her whether fhe
had ever been with him any where elfe? to which fhe
anfwered, Yes; and added, that fhe went with Mr.
Chamberlain to his warehoufe in White Lion-ftreet on
the Saturday following, where he again committed adultery with her, or words to that effect.

The same witness, examined on interrogatories, said, that she did neither know or believe that Mr. Timmings committed adultery with any loose woman, and thereby contract the veneral disease; but, on the contrary, had heard him declare that he had it of his wife, Mrs. Ann Timmings.

Thomas Mountfort, of Moon Yard, Shoreditch, a journeyman weaver, affirmed, that being acquainted with the proceedings of Mr. Smith and Mrs. Timmings, and being in the habit of going of errands and the like for her husband, in consequence of some conversation with Thomas Gillett, his fellow-witness, upon the subject, he was set by him to watch them in the yard into which the kitchen window opened; this was on the evening of the 10th of January. Through a crevice in the same he could see almost every thing that passed, he then observed, that on the maid's going out and leaving James Smith and Mrs. Timmings by themselves, Smith took and kissed her, and put his hands up her petticoats several times; in a short time after, Smith got up from his chair, and he saw them both move towards the window, Mrs. Timmings moving in her chair; when they came quite close to the window he could not see particularly what passed, any further than that Smith was upon her, and that both their bodies were in motion for some minutes; after which he saw Mr. Smith get up and sit in the chair he was in before. He then left them, and informed Gillett of what had passed.

On the 12th of January, it seems only two days after, about eight in the evening, Gillett came again to him and informed him that Mr. Smith was there, and further desired him to resume his old station—He did so, and through the same crevice observed that the maid-servant went out as before; and as Mrs. Timmings and Mr. Smith then sat opposite to him, he could very well see what passed; he then very plainly observed Smith put his left arm round her neck, and while she laid her head upon his shoulders, he put his right hand up her petticoats and after remaining so about a minute, he got up, and having unbuttoned his breeches, the witness plainly saw him pull up her petticoats so far, that while he placed himself between her thighs, he could plainly see them naked on each side of him. He then again observed their bodies in motion.

But what is the most remarkable, while the witness was in this situation, Mr. Timmings, who was privy to his being placed there, occasionly came into the yard, and asked him if he had seen any thing indecent between the parties? It was about nine o'clock when Mr. Timmings first came to him upon this curious enquiry. He after came again at the critical moment, when Smith was placing himself upon his wife, which he took a view of through the crevice; and immediately after going and opening the kitchen-door, he went up to Smith, pushed him off his wife, called him a villain, asked him what business he had there, and afterwards turned him out of the house——He then called Gillett, and told him to go and fetch Mrs. Timmings, his mother——Gillett, on Smith's getting up from Mrs. Timmings, observed that the flap of his breeches was quite down.

As a case in point, and something relevelant to Mr. Timmings's patient waiting at the kitchen-window to see the completion of Mr. Smith's amour with Mrs. Timmings, we must mention a Benedict, or rather a Jerry Sneak, in the neighbourhood of Barbican, who used to be sent for liquor while a visitor of his wife's was left alone with her. When he returned from these errands, upon being let into the apartment, he would frequently say, " he had been at the door a good while!" nd if he was asked by his wife and her gallant why he did not come in? his reply was, " Because I thought you might be *busy*!"

To a further interrogation, the witness said, that on the night of the 12th of January Mrs. Timmings said to her husband, Pray forgive me this time, and I'll do so no more! and that he never heard her make any other confession whatever. To this he added, that no threats or promisses were made use of to extort it from her at that time.   Of her difpofition, he added it as his opinion, that fhe is a woman of fuch a fimple and unfufpicious turn, that any artful perfon might eafily make her declare what had never occurred.

Mary Gibbs, fervant to Mr. Daniel Timmings, faid, that foon after fhe came to live there fhe ufed to obferve a man, a ftranger, to her, come backwards and forwards to the houfe in Union-ftreet, whom her miftrefs afterwards told her was a Mr. James Barbett, a perfon who fhe knew before fhe was married, and had been her fweetheart.   About three weeks after this witnefs came to live there, fhe recollects carrying a note to him from Mrs Timmings to where Mr. Barbett lived, in Stewart-ftreet near Union-ftreet.   From that time till the 13th of January laft fhe carried feveral notes to the fame perfon from her miftrefs, in confequence of which he came to the houfe feveral evenings, but always when Mr. Timmings was abfent, and would ftay with Mrs. Timmings half or three quarters of an hour at a time : at thefe times Mr. Barbett and her miftrefs were generally alone in the parlour on the ground-floor, and fhe frequently heard him kifs her when he went away.   Another time, as they were in the kitchen, fhe faw him put his arm round her waift and upon her breaft, and obferved that her handkerchief appeared tumbled; this was at a time when fhe had left them together near three quarters of an hour. After Mr. Barbett was gone away, her miftrefs told her, that if ever any thing fhould happen, and fhe and Mr. Timmings fhould part, Mr. Barbett had repeatedly promifed to take care of her.   Another time, after returning from a walk on the Hackney road, fhe told this witnefs that Mr. Barbett and fhe had been and eaten cheefe-cakes together at a houfe on the way, and that he had affured her he would never forfake her !—Simplicity with a witnefs !—And, as a further proof of this difpofition, according to the teftimony of Mary Gibbs, the confidant, Mr. Barbett was once going by the door, and being called into the parlour by Mr. Timmings to examine him about his connection with Mrs. Timmings,

Barbett said to her, Did I ever know you ? to which she immediately replied, Yes, Sir, you know you did, this very night four weeks, on this very carpet! stamping her foot upon the place at the same time. She then went into the kitchen, where Mrs. Amey Barker and the deponent then were, when addressing herself to them, she said, Though he denies it here, he can't deny it in a court of justice ; she then laughed, and the conversation ended for that night. The next night, it seems, Mrs. Barker, and Mrs. Grace Timmings being present, the latter said to Mrs. Timmings, " How can I ask my son to forgive you, when you know you have been that wicked woman before ? and proceeded thus : " Nancy, who was it that gave you the bad distemper ? was it Mr. Barbett or Mr. Carre ?" to which she replied, " It was Mr. Barbett ." and being further asked what she took for it ? she answered, Bitter aloes, jalap, and brandy. And further this witness could not depose.

But to another article she answered, that Mr. J. Smith came to their house sometimes twice a day, and that one night going away about 10 o'clock, he kissed Mrs. Timmings twice ; they also tickled one another, but on his putting his hand upon her breast, she immediately desired this witness, the maid, to put the wine upon the table, and go upon an errand, which she accordingly did, and left them together till 12 o'clock.

From her testimony it also appeared, that on the 12th of January, when Mrs. Timmings's connection was discovered with Mr. Smith, Mr Timmings had talked of going to Greenwich, but returned home unexpectedly, after being absent about half an hour. On the maid's opening the door to him, seeing him confused, she asked him what was the matter ? in answer, he desired her to go and ask her mistress ; she then went into the kitchen and found her mistress with Mrs. Grace Timmings and her fellow-witness, Thomas Mount—her mistress was then crying, and said to her in the presence of all the company, " I have committed adultery with Mr. Smith, and your master has turned him out of doors !"

Amey Barker, wife of Edward Barker, a master in his Majesty's navy, in Paradise-Row, Rotherhithe, deposed, that she well knew James Barbett, by seeing him several times at Mr. Timmings's house in Union-street : and that one night in December 1790, in particular, she saw a light in the window of the back parlour, on which she supposed Mr. Timmings had company that might be strangers to her ; on this supposition she went up to the window, and as there was a vacancy between the shutters, she could plainly see every part of the room, and, to her great surprize, then saw Ann Timmings laying upon the carpet, her petticoats were drawn quite up, and a man laying upon her, in this situation they continued some minutes, during which she is certain she saw their bodies move, and was well convinced they had a mutual knowledge of each other in a carnal way.   And in confirmation of this idea, she afterwards observed James Barbett button up his breeches, and Ann Timmings go and sit down in a chair in a very pensive manner ; but as she heard somebody coming along the street, she left the place, and returned to her sister's.

It was also her opinion, that Mr. Timmings had contracted the venereal disease from no other person but his wife, and she was fully persuaded that he had never treated her with cruelty or violence.

But still the most surprising part of this evidence was, that Mrs. Amey Barker deposed, that Mrs. Timmings was a woman of such a pliable and unsuspicious disposition, as very easily to be imposed upon ; and seemingly as a proof of this asseveration, the next part of the deposition that followed, expressed that James Barbett and Ann Timmings had absolutely committed adultery together, about the 15th of the month of December 1790, upon Mrs. Timmings's parlour-floor in Duke-street, while she, Mrs. Barker, was sitting at the window between seven and eight o'clock in the evening. This transaction, she observed, she never informed Mr. Timmings of, but added, that he spoke of it to her about the latter end of January laft, which was the firft time fhe was apprifed of his knowing of it !

Mary Gibbs alfo depofed, that Mr. and Mrs. Timmings and Mr. Smith all fupped together one night; and that afterwards about ten o'clock Mr. Timmings went out and left Smith and his wife together a confiderable time; during which, fhe was witnefs to their ufual intimacies of kiffing, and the like.

But this, though the concluding part of the evidence, was not the only appearance of connivance, to fay nothing of Mrs Barker's prefence during the parlour-floor fcene. A caufe of this kind brought on, where enormous damages were alfo obtained, would in fome fenfe account for the palpable fcenes of intricate expofure all the way through . but as this muft have terminated, it is very evident there was in reality Much to do about Nothing.

The Judge very properly refufed to divorce the parties.

The Trial of James Lavander, at the Seffions-Houfe, Old Bailey, for a Rape upon the Body of Mary Lewis, Spinfter, and robbing her of Half a Guinea. —April 1793.

ANN LEWIS fworn. I am fourteen years and three months old.

Court. Remember you are now going to give an account of a tranfaction which may effect the life of the prifoner at the bar; let me caution you to fpeak the truth and nothing but the truth.

Ann Lewis.   On Friday the 22d of March, I lived a fervant at Mr. M'Carty's, the Beehive, in Nightingale-lane; I came there the Wednefday before, and this tranfaction happened on the Friday morning.

Q. Where did you live before this ?—At Mr. Stagoths, the Nag's Head, Poftern-row, Little Tower-hill.

Q. Is the Beehive a houfe of reputation, or is it a houfe where men and women come ?—It is.

Q. Is it a houfe of good reputation, or is it a houfe of ill fame, that receives all forts of men and women ?—All forts of men and women come there.

Q. Do the loofe women come there ?—Yes.

Q. Who placed you as a fervant there ?—Mr. Carty's other girl came to my mother, and told her they wanted a maid.   I hired myfelf there; my mother was bad in bed: my mother knew I hired myfelf there; fhe lived about four doors off, where fhe had lived but a fortnight, and I had been in the neighbourhood but two days.   On the 20th of March, Wednefday night, when I went there the firft night, the prifoner was drinking along with Mrs. Carty, and he laid hold of me, and faid I was a pretty girl; I told him to keep his hands to himfelf: I faw him again the next day in the fame houfe, when he laid hold of me, and I again told him to keep his hands to himfelf; Mrs. Carty laughed at it.   The next day he came again, and ordered half a pint of gin to go upon Bunker's-hill; he did not live there, I did not know the houfe; my miftrefs called me out of the wafh-houfe, and fent me with it.   I followed him with the gin; he went into a houfe; I went to the door, and I faid Here is the gin: there was a woman in the room, (I ftaid at the door, the door was open) and the table before her, and there was a tea-cup on the table; I

gave him the half-pint of gin, and the woman said,
Come in here, my dear, there is nobody here will
hurt you.   I did not go any further than the door
all the time.   I was waiting for the meafure ; he
took the gin out of my hand at the door.   Mrs.
Carty told me to bring the meafure back again, or
take notice where it was going, as it was a ftrange
houfe.   The woman got up and laid hold of me to
pull me in, and pufhed me in, and faid I am going
for a farthing-worth of thread, and fhe would be in
in a minute.   I laid hold of her to go after her,
and fhe would not let me, fhe pufhed me in and pulled the door after her, and this man came and locked the door, and put the key in his pocket; and he
laid hold of me, and there was a bureau bed-ftead
in the room, and he laid hold of one of my hands,
and he was going to pull the bedftead down ; with
that I fcreamed out, and he took his hat off and put
it on my face ; there was fomething in the hat that
catched me, that ftrangled me, that preffed on my
throat ! I had a half guinea in my pocket, that my
mother gave me in the morning ; I told him I
would give it him if he would let me go : this was
juft as he was going to put the hat on my face.   No,
by Chrift ! fays he, I will have my revenge of you
now ; he had a great coat on, he wrapped it round
me and flung me down on the floor ; he put fomething in my private parts that cut me: I was covered all the while.

Q. Was it far in your private parts ?—Yes it
was.

Q. When you fay it cut you, do you mean a fharp
inftrument ; or that it tore your private parts ?—
It tore them.

Q. And he lay his body on your's ?—Yes, he did.

Q. How long did he lay on you ?—I cannot right-
ly fay.   I fainted away in the hat ; when I recovered, I was laying on the floor ; he was on me ftill ;

he get off from me then; and when I got up, I found myself all blood.

Q. On what part of your body?—All my shift and my private parts; I never had been before this out of order

Q. Do you mean you never had those discharges which are common to your sex?—I never had before: he then opened the door, and I was going out; when I recovered myself, he pulled me back again; says he, Where is the half guinea you was going to give a while ago? I told him, if he had let me go, I would have given it him then: he said, I have had your maidenhead, and I will have that too; he then laid hold and pulled my pocket off from my side; from the pull he gave it, I thought my back was broke in two; he took my pocket and all there was in it, a red pocket-book; he kept all that was in the pocket: the half guinea was in the pocket, in the pocket-book: there was also a pocket-book in it, and a pair of scissars, and two-pence half-penny in copper, three of them crooked, and two farthings; and when I came home to Mrs. Carty's, I could hardly walk. I went backwards and washed myself. I went out with a pint of beer afterwards, and I went to my mother, but she was not at home. I went out about fifteen minutes afterwards, and went again several times that day, and she was not at home; I saw her that night; she was in bed, it was about seven o'clock she looked out of the window, but she could not come down; I told her I wanted to speak to her very particularly. I was in the court, and I called to her; the window opens into the court: she told me to come in the morning, because my father was asleep: the next day I went ab-ut eight o'clock in the morning; she was in bed, I went up stairs to her, and I told her what had happened: she asked me if I told my master, I told her I had not, because of my character;

fhe gave me fome cloths ; I got well about a week ago.

Q. How long was it kept fecret between you and your mother ?—About a week and a day over ; the Juftice fent for the doctor of the London Hofpital, and he faid I had the bad diftemper.

Prifoner. I hope you will enquire into her character and her mother's.

Mary Barrett fworn. I am the mother of the laft witnefs. I am married to my fecond hufband.

Q. How long had your daughter been at fervice ?—She never was out but a twelvemonth, and fhe lived with Mr. Stagold, Poftern-row, thefe twelve months; fhe is fourteen years old laft Chriftmas ; fhe went to Carty's fervice the Wednefday night before this happened.

Q. How long did you know Carty before your daughter was placed in this fervice ?—I did not know them at all; I came down from living in Whitechapel into this houfe, where I am at prefent.

Q. Had you made any enquiry into the character of Carty's houfe, or did you know what kind of a houfe it was ?—The maid that lives at Carty's, called at my houfe for pots, and fhe afked me if my girl wanted a place, my being ill at the fame time ; I faid that I would not wifh her to go and live in that houfe, a public-houfe, efpecially an Irifh houfe. The next day fhe called again, and fhe faid fhe had fpoke to her miftrefs, and fhe faid fhe would be very glad if my daughter would come to live with her. H. ving been very ill, and having five children, the youngeft fix years old, and this prefent man not their father, I told the girl to go after it for a little time, till I got better, and I would get her into a private houfe ; fhe went after it and hired herfelf, and was to have four guineas a year, and that morning fhe was hired ; I was going to the hofpital, and I gave her the half guinea to pay for her fhoes foleing and heel-piecing.

Q. What was your complaint ?—It was in my head ; I have had several blisters, and I have been in the hospital ten months, and two of my children along with me.

Q. How did you procure this half guinea, as you was a poor woman ?—I had been saving it to buy a gown, so put by half a crown a week unknown to my husband. I saved it to buy the children something.

Q. Do you recollect where you was during the Friday ?—I was down at an acquaintance of mine, being so very ill, and she kept me to drink a dish of tea, and I could hardly crawl home at six o'clock.

Q. What was your acquaintance's name ?—Her name is Mrs. Smith, she lives in Cartwright-street in that neighbourhood ; and I came home, and my husband came directly after me, and I laid down directly, being so very ill, and he had a bit of supper and laid down before eight o'clock ; we were all in bed before eight o'clock, children and all.

Q. Where does your bedchamber window look to ?—It looks into the court ; there is but four houses in the court. The girl knocked at the door soon after I was in bed, before eight, between seven and eight ; I heard her call, and I went to the window, and she said she wanted to speak to me very particularly ; I told her I was very ill, and her father was asleep, and she must come in the morning, and I would hear what she had got to say ; she called on me the next morning about eight o'clock, and shewed me herself, and told me what had happened to her the day before, and I asked her if she told her master ? she said no, on account of her character ; I then told her not to do it ; and I asked her what sort of a fellow it was ? she said it was an ill looking fellow in sailor's clothes ; I said, Don't speak to any body about it till I get better ; and I got a little better.

Q. Did you tell your husband of it ?—I did not,

upon my word, becaufe he is the fecond father ; my hufband is a hard working man.

Q. In what manner does your prefent hufband behave to this child by your firft hufband ?—Very fond of her, but not altogether as if he was her own father.

Q. Why did not you tell him ?—I did not tell him indeed. As foon as I could crawl out of doors I went to Mr. Dawfon the officer, this was on Saturday, 7, 8, or 9, days after, I told it to Mr. Dawfon ; he is a peace-officer, his wife was prefent, he is here now.

Q. Did you on the day on which your daughter called on you, examine the ftate in which fhe was ? —I did ; fhe was all over bloody, her private parts all torn, and her fhift all over bloody.

Prifoner. I want to know how this poor woman could come by the half guinea to give her daughter.

Court. I have afked her that.

Prifoner. How often did your daughter go out of nights ?—She never went out of nights,

Court to Mrs. Barett. I afk, on your folemn oath, whether this girl behaved with decency and modefty before fhe went to Carty's houfe ?—She did, upon my oath, the fame as my youngeft child, if I never enter the kingdom of Heaven.

Q. Had you any reafon to fuppofe fhe had been debauched before ?—No.

Q. Had you ever obferved any thing wanton or unfeemly in her behaviour ?—No, never.

Q. Had the girl any monthly difcharges before this time ?—Never no more than a fucking baby ; fhe now does not know what to do, fhe has got the bad diftemper fo bad.

Thomas Bently *fworn*—I am a furgeon, I attend at the London Hofpital. I was defired to examine the girl on Friday, I believe it was the day fhe was at the Juftice's. I found a confiderable degree of

x

inflammation and discharge of matter from her private parts.

Q. Had she contracted any bad disease?—There was the appearance, but I cannot tell whether the inflammation proceeded from violence or from the venereal disease; there was a deal of redness?

Court to Mrs. Barrett. Has any other medical gentleman attended her since she was examined by Mr. Bentl?—No.

Q. Why did not you apply to some medical person? why did not you take her to the hospital?—The Justice promised me that he would give her something to take.

Prisoner. Before I speak, I wish Mr. Dawson to go out of Court.

We made the agreement to take the half pint of gin to Bunker's-hill, the girl and I; there were two men present; the mistress sent the other maid to go with it, and she said, "O, I will go with it!" accordingly she did: when we came to the house, the door was latched, I took and drawed the spring of the latch, and came in; and as soon as I came in, I gave the woman in the room a glass of gin, and told her I would pay her for the use of the room: she went out and stood on the stairs while the business was done. I took and laid her down on the boards and pulled up her petticoats, and the tail of her smock was as stiff as parchment, several different colours: when she found I was feeling the tail of her smock she whips her hand round, and takes it on one side; I had drank very hard, I could not execute my office properly, I could not get it to stand, so she called me a fumbler several times; at last I coaxed it up, and got it to stand, and got in; when it was over, she takes the quartern measure, and was going, Stop, says I, the gin is not all drank so I gave her some: she went home, and I followed and went into the tap-room. I sat one side of the fire, she would pass up and down to the bar, and as she passed she would say, O you fumbler ! these two men were sitting in the tap-room with me. I called for a quart of beer and quartern of gin, and she drank a glass of it ; after I came out of the house, I went down to the water side to work at the rigging along the shore ; I earned two shillings that night. I came home, and sitting in the tap-room, and then she wanted me to get clear of the other woman I live with, and live along with her ; she even wanted me to go to Ireland with her, and she told me her mother had a bed to let, and she wanted me to go and live along with her at her mother's. Mr. Dawson put her up to this a fortnight after it happened : Mr. Dawson is her landlord.

Court. Do you choose to ask Mr. Dawson any questions ?—No. Mr. Dawson took me out of the room.

Q. What do you impute to Mr. Dawson ?—Impute to Mr. Dawson that he has done something improper ; he was the officer that took me.

Q What did Mr Dawson do that is improper ? —He has urged her and her mother up to all this.

Mr. Dawson called in and sworn—I am a constable.

Q It is supposed that this prosecution has been carried on by your advice ?—When the mother and girl applied to me at my own house, I took them immediately to a magistrate I did advise her to prosecute the man, and I advised her to go to the magistrate.

Court. Did any thing pass to induce you to conceive in any shape that this was an imposition on you ?—Nothing in the world.

Q Are you that woman's landlord ?—I am not.

Jeremiah Leonard sworn—I was at Mr Carty's house, I cannot say the day of the month, but it was Friday, the prisoner was there : Cullen and I came into the house, and called for a pot of beer, and sat

down in the box ; the prisoner at the bar came and
sat along with us for a little while, he then got up
again, and this young woman and he began to joke
and play together and kiss one another while we
were drinking ; at last they began to whisper and
joke together ; what they said I cannot tell, but he
came to us and told us he was going to have a stroke
at her, and so on, and called for a pint of gin, and
she and he went out together, she carried the gin ;
then we waited till they both came back again ;
she came in first, and she had a bit of a blush like ;
he came in afterwards in less than a minute and a
half or couple of minutes, I am very particular in
what I say, one or another is nothing to me.

Q. Did you observe any thing in her countenance
when she came in ?—I took a little notice ?—however, when he came after, he came to her and kissed her, and called for another quartern of gin, and
drank part of it, and she drank with him by the
fire-side where her mistress could not see her ; he
brought the remainder of the gin to us in the box,
and told us that he had a do with her ; we drank
the gin, and he gave us the pot of beer besides. I
have known this man a matter of four years, he lodged with me.

Q. Being used to frequent Carty's house, did you
make no observations concerning his saying, He
would have to do with this young girl ?—I did not
say any thing against it.

Q. How many people were in the tap-room when
he and the girl went out first ?—John Cullen and I
were in one box, there is a table in the box.

Q. Did you both sit on one side of the table ?—I
cannot say.

Q. Did any body sit at the same table with you ?
—No.

Q. Which of you came into the tap-room first,
you or Cullen?—I came in first, I was in before
Cullen.

Q. Was any body in company with Cullen?—He came alone.

Q. Did you stay in the house all the time this prisoner a d girl was about?—Yes; they seemed both very agreeable when they came back, kissing one another and joking, so with that he gave us a pot of beer, and when they returned, they sat by the fire-side, where her mistress could not see.

Q Did he sit down in any box at all?—No, he came to us and told us that he had stroked her.

Thomas Carey—I have known the prisoner at the bar about five months.

Q Is he a married man or a single man?—He has got a company keeper.

Prisoner. I am not married.

Carey. I never saw nothing by him but civility : one night I was going in for a pint of beer for my supper, and I met with this young woman going out with a pot of beer from Carty's as I was going in, and she told me to send James Lavander after her ; this was four or five days before he was taken up ; I told him, says he, Damn her, it will not do.

Court to Mrs. Barrett. I think it was the day after this Friday that your daughter told you : did you suffer your daughter to continue at Carty's afterward?—She did not come away till the Saturday after that. I told her to stop there till I got better, because I had been very ill ; this here man that is gone down now, his wife came to my house and I asked her what she wanted? she said she wanted me to make it up with Lavander, and these Irish people would make a subscription, and give me some guineas.

Prisoner. I could not stay in the tap-room to take a pint of beer but what she would be sending out somebody to me to come and meet her : the most common place we met at was in Brown Bear Alley, and when I would not meet her, she would look sulky, and I often went out and did not do any execution : this was the way I had this connection with her.

The prisoner called two witnesses to his character.

Leonard to Court. Ask the girl whether she did not take up with a man before on such a charge, who lived in the Minories.

Ann Lewis. No, never.

Q. Nor your mother.

Guilty, Death ! Aged 28. Tried by the first Middlesex Jury, before Lord Kenyon.

The extraordinary Trial between Lady Elizabeth Weld and her husband, Edward Weld, Esq. for Impotency, In the Arches Court of Canterbury, London; 1732.

THE counsel for the prosecution stated, that Edward Weld Esq married the Honourable Catharine Elizabeth, daughter of Lord Aston, June 22, 1727, he being aged 22, and the lady 19. That after his marriage he cohabited with his wife at his seat at Lulworth Castle, in Dorsetshire, till June, 1728, excepting one month, wherein, being indisposed, she came to London for advice, from whence she went to the seat of her father, at Standon, in Hertfordshire, where her husband followed her in the October following, and cohabited with her about a month, and then returned to Lulworth, where he continued till February 1728-9, and came back to his wife at her father's seat, and staid with her about three weeks, he then left her there a second time, and went home to Lulworth Castle, and continued there till the end of May following, and then returned to her again for one week; after which they both came to London, and cohabited as man and wife about six weeks. During all those times of cohabitation, she said, he never (by reason of impotency) consummated his marriage, though he acknowledged her to be able, apt, and fit for the pro-creation of children · his wife, therefore, would no longer cohabit with him, though urged by him to it, by his tell-ing her that "Many married people had lived together like brother and sister."—To which she replied, "My dear, we ought not to live together after this manner!"

All our fair readers will agree with Mrs. Weld, that a married state ought to be quite another manner of life from that of brother and sister, and the lady must be esteemed blameless in commencing this suit, as she was herself, and her husband likewise, a Roman Catholic; especially, as by their religion, matrimony is looked up-on to be a sacrament—And t is further understood by those of that persuasion, that this sacrament is violated by such as continue in the married state while they are con-scious to themselves that they cannot answer the holy ends of its institution.

The counsel then produced Lord Aston, who deposed, that Mr Weld and Mr. Colclough being at his house in Hertfordshire, in May 1728; he desired Mr. Colclough to speak to Mr. Weld about his Not having consummated the marriage with his daughter. Mr Colclough declared he had spoke to him, and he confessed he had Not con-summated his marriage with the said Mrs Weld, and that he had some outward defect that was painful to him, and hindered him from consummating his marriage. Mr. Colclough then recommended one Mr. Williams to Mr. Weld, who had cured him of a similar disorder; and after this it seems, Mr. Weld told the witness at the lady Howard's, that Mr. Williams had cured him, though that some soreness remained, but he did not doubt but he should be well in a little time.

The Duke of Norfolk depofed, that in June 1748, when he talked to Mr. Weld about the affair, he acknowledged he had not confummated his marriage with the Honourable Mifs Afton, but had advifed with phyficians and hoped in a little time he fhould be able to confummate it.

The fubftance of the certificate of three midwives was then produced, it was as follows ——" That they are well fkilled in the art and practice of midwifery, and have very carefully and diligently infpected the private parts of the body of the Hon. Catharine Elizabeth Weld, which are naturally defigned for carnal copulation, and that to the beft of their fkill and knowledge fhe is a *Virgin*, and never had carnal copulation with any man whatfoever.

ELIZABETH FISHER,
REBECCA MANN,
MARY BAKER.

The following Depofitions were made in behalf of the Defendant——

Edward Weld, Efq. depofed, that he was of the age of 20, and has all the parts of his body which conftitute a man perfect and entire, *more particularly thofe parts* which nature formed for the propagation of his fpecies and the act of carnal copulation, in full and juft proportion, and was and is capable of carnally knowing Catharine Elizabeth Weld, his wife, or any other woman. And that during the time he cohabited with his wife, his privy-member was often *turgid, dilated, and erected*, as was neceffary to perform the act of carnal copulation, and that he did at fuch times confumate his marriage by carnally lying with and knowing his wife.

Margaret Weld, the mother of Mrs. Weld, depofed, that within the fpace of a twelvemonth, or thereabouts, after the folemnization of the marriage between her fon and the Hon Mifs Afton, that her daughter-in-law being out of order, as breeding women ufually are, informed the witnefs that fhe did not know for certain that fhe was not a breeding!

Mr. Williams, an eminent furgeon, depofed, that Mr. Weld came to him in June 1728, and that upon examining his penis, he found the frenum too ftraight, which he fet at liberty by cliping it with a pair of fciffars, and on examining that part again the next day, found nothing amifs in the organs of generation.

The following was then read, being the fubftance of the certificate of five furgeons that had examined the Defendant:

" That they had carefully infpected the parts of Edward Weld, Efq defigned for propagation, and did find them fully and juftly proportioned, and fitly formed for the act of carnal copulation, and that it did evidently appear to them that he was capable of performing every thing requifite to the propagation of his fpecies."

> A DICKENS, Serjt. Surgeon.
> C. AMYAND,
> W CHESSELDEN,
> A SMALL,
> W. GREEN.

The Court having heard the above evidence, decreed that Mrs. Weld fhould be enjoined to *perpetual filence* on thefe premifes, and that fhe fhould go and cohabit with her hufband at bed and board at Lulworth Caftle, or any other place of his abode.

After this fentence, there was an appeal to the King in his Court of Delegates. The caufe was re-heard at Serjeant's Inn, and the foregoing fentence was confirmed!

To which we may very fafely venture to add, without fear of being guilty of a libel, that to impofe a fentence of perpetual filence upon a woman, for its cruelty and injuftice never before had any parrallel in the annals or law books of any chriftian country whatever!

CONTENTS.

CONTENTS.

CONTENTS.

Lightning Source UK Ltd.
Milton Keynes UK
UKHW031229200319
339513UK00005B/611/P

9 781274 885784